PERSUASION POINTS

82 Strategic Exercises for Writing High-Scoring Persuasive Essays

BRIAN BACKMAN

Persuasion Points: 82 Strategic Exercises for Writing High-Scoring Persuasive Essays

Cover design, book layout, and design: Studio Montage
Editors: Tiffany Morgan/Kendall M. Sharp

Library of Congress Cataloging-in-Publication Data
Backman, Brian.
     Persuasion points : 82 strategic exercises for writing high-scoring persuasive essays / Brian Backman.
          p. cm.
     Includes bibliographical references and index.
     ISBN-13: 978-1-934338-77-3
1. English language--writing--Study and teaching. 2. English language--Rhetoric--Study and teaching.
3. English teachers--Training of--United States. I. Title.
          PE1404.B24 2010
808'.0420712--dc22
                                                          2010015504

Maupin House publishes professional resources for K-12 educators. Contact us for
tailored, in-school training or to schedule an author for a workshop or conference.
Visit www.maupinhouse.com for free lesson plan downloads.

 Maupin House

Maupin House Publishing, Inc.
2416 N.W. 71st Place
Gainesville, FL 32653
www.maupinhouse.com
800-524-0634
352-373-5588
352-373-5546 (fax)
info@maupinhouse.com

10   9   8   7   6   5   4   3   2   1

Dedication

For

Joy, Sam, and Max

TABLE OF CONTENTS

INTRODUCTION

PART I: Style Points Persuasive Exercises for Student Practice   1

STRATEGY #1:   Ideas and Details—Build a Strong Structural Foundation 2
     Overview 2

     CHAPTER 1:   Claims and Premises—The Rhetorical Rod and Reel 4
         1.   Logic Meets Duct Tape 7
         2.   The Two Parts of a Thesis 8
         3.   Thesis Under Construction 9
         4.   The Claim Game 10
         5.   Build Your Ethos with Counterarguments 11
         6.   Television: Terrific or Terrible? 13
         7.   Transitions: Transportation You Need 14
         8.   Not Your Average Writing Assignment 15
         Teaching Notes and Answers 16

     CHAPTER 2:   Examples—Tell and Show 21
         9.   Two Important Words 24
        10. Persuading with the Three Appeals:
             Logos, Pathos, and Ethos 25
        11. Using Details to Persuade:
             Statistics, Dialogue, and Quotations 26
        12. Organizing with Examples .27
        13. Anecdotes: The Secret Is Out! 28
        14. Inductive Hook and Full-circle Conclusion 29
        15. What, Why, and How 31
        16. Take the Inductive Challenge 32
        17. Story Time 33
        18. Signs of the Specific Kind 35
         Teaching Notes and Answers 36

STRATEGY #2: Diction and Tone—Choose Words That Support the Thesis 42

    Overview 42

CHAPTER 3: Vivid Verbs—Video and Volume 44

    19. The Sights and Sounds of Verbs 47
    20. Add Pictures and Sound 48
    21. Passive Resistance 49
    22. Zeugma: Last but Not Least 50
    23. Vivid Verbs, Not Verbosity .51
    24. Virtue with Verbs 52
    25. I Need Some Advice! 53

    Teaching Notes and Answers .54

CHAPTER 4: Concrete Nouns—Knee-high Tube Socks,
a Brown Bag, and a Splash of Salt Water 58

    26. Pouring Concrete 61
    27. The Ladder of Abstraction .62
    28. Abstract to Concrete 63
    29. Concrete Hook and Full-circle Conclusion 64
    30. Wish You Were Here 65
    31. The Big Hassle 66
    32. Horoscope Hilarity 67

    Teaching Notes and Answers .68

CHAPTER 5: Lists—The Parade of Particulars 71

    33. Listmania 73
    34. Asyndeton and Polysyndeton 74
    35. Hyphenated Modifier 75
    36. In Praise of … 76
    37. Defining Abstractions 77
    38. Chamber of Commerce Description 78

    Teaching Notes and Answers .79

STRATEGY #3: Figurative Language—Use Compelling Comparisons 82

    Overview 82

CHAPTER 6: Metaphor and Simile—Old Ideas Made New 84

    39. Metaphorically Speaking 87
    40. Creating Fresh Metaphors .88
    41. Explicit and Implicit Metaphors 89
    42. Figurative-language Hook and Full-circle Conclusion .90
    43. Commemoration 91
    44. The Glass Is Half-full 92
    45. Life Is a Metaphor 93

    Teaching Notes and Answers .94

CHAPTER 7: Personification—It's Alive 97

    46. Personification: Bring Words to Life 99
    47. Personification in Practice 100
    48. Abstractions in the Flesh 101
    49. Time Flies 102
    50. Make Your Toothpaste Sing .103
    51. I Am the Textbook, I Make You Work 104

    Teaching Notes and Answers .105

CHAPTER 8: Allusions—Name Dropping 108

    52. What's in a Name? 111
    53. Allusions: From Story to Idea 112
    54. Speaking Figuratively 113
    55. Grade A Allusions 114
    56. Cell Phones 115
    57. Allusion Meets Advertising 116

    Teaching Notes and Answers .117

STRATEGY #4: Syntax—Write Sentences That Are Clear,
Varied, and Rhythmic 122

    Overview 122

CHAPTER 9: Parallelism—Three-peat After Me 124

    58. Parallel Lines 127
    59. Parallelism in Action 128
    60. Tribute 129
    61. PSA 130
    62. Parallel Previews 131

    Teaching Notes and Answers .132

CHAPTER 10: Antithesis—Opposites Attract 134

    63. Spot the Antithesis 137
    64. Proverbial Antithesis 138
    65. Balanced Antithesis 139
    66. Claiming a Contrast 140
    67. Focused Contrast 141
    68. Four-word Dramatic Dialogue 142

    Teaching Notes and Answers .143

CHAPTER 11: Alliteration and Anaphora—You Can Say That Again . 145

    69.   Repetition for a Reason 148
    70.   Echoing Words and Sounds 150
    71.   Reruns Worth Watching: Alliteration and Anaphora . 151
    72.   One Change. 152
    73.   Overrated/Underrated 153
    74.   Composition Replete with Repetitive T's 154
    75.   Alliterative Antithesis Hook and Full-circle Conclusion 155

    Teaching Notes and Answers 156

CHAPTER 12: Sentence Variety—The Long and the Short of It 160

    76.   Revise for Variety...Out Loud. 163
    77.   Sentence Smorgasbord: Cumulative and Periodic . . . 164
    78.   I Came, I Saw, I Balanced 165
    79.   What's the Difference? 166
    80.   Best of the Web. 167
    81.   Radio Readers 168
    82.   Lessons from Fiction or Film. 169

    Teaching Notes and Answers 170

STYLE POINTS QUIZ. 174

STYLE POINTS QUIZ ANSWERS 178

PART II: Putting the Essay Together   179

CHAPTER 13: Guiding Students through the Writing Process 180

    Step 1: Pre-writing and Writing a Conclusion and the First Draft 180
        Pre-writing for a Point: Student Scaffold 182
        Conclusions: How Does it All End? 183
    Step 2: Revising for Coherence and Organization 184
        Keeping It Coherent: Comparing Essays. 185
        Signal Words: Three Techniques for Coherent Writing 188
        Pointing the Way: Self Revision and Peer Revision. . . 189
    Step 3: Editing for the Correct Use of Conventions 193
        Editing Checklist. 194

    Teaching Notes 195

CHAPTER 14: Problem-solving and Assessment. 198

    Pinpointing Problems: Matching Rubrics with the Strategies 198
    Scoring Essays with a Rubric 201
    Six-point Writing Rubric. 207

    Teaching Notes 208

CHAPTER 15: Extra Skill-sharpening Games and Activities for the Whole Class. 210

    Strategy Points: The Game 211
    Collaborative Writing Activity: Tone for Two 214

PART III: Resources. 217

STUDENT HANDOUT: REVIEW AND REVISION REMINDERS. 218

101 WRITING PROMPTS. 225

GLOSSARY OF KEY TERMS. 229

PROFESSIONAL RESOURCES. 232

INTRODUCTION

Now more than ever, the well-developed persuasive essay has become a major instructional focal point for the high-school English teacher. Classroom writing assignments and assessments have long required good persuasive essays.

Increasingly, however, Advanced Placement exams, state assessments, the College Board, and the new SAT demand strong persuasive essays, too. These high-stakes essay exams require students to state a clear point and support it with sufficient evidence and explanation. They require students to balance reason and imagination to produce essays that stand out from the crowd.

Style is the component of writing that creates the stand-out essay. As used in this resource, the word "style" refers to four key strategies that all good persuasive writers must use. They begin with a strong structural foundation, first crafting a strong and logical claim and premise. They support their theses with appropriate diction: examples, vivid verbs, and concrete examples, manipulating their words for specificity and effect.

Strong persuasive writers use appropriate figurative language, those compelling comparisons and allusions that bring a piece to life and make for interesting reading.

Finally, they add syntax techniques, making sure their sentences are clear, varied, and rhythmic. Their deliberate choice of techniques like parallelism, antithesis, alliteration, and anaphora add a deeper dimension to their arguments and further enhance the pleasure of reading their essays.

The components of style are no great mystery. Too often, unfortunately, it's the missing component in student writing, and teachers are often at a loss as to how to teach it, especially given time and curricular constraints.

This professional resource and idea book is designed to provide teachers with the background, instructional knowledge, and student exercises they need to help students make the leap from adequate to outstanding persuasive essays. With these points, students gain practice with strategies that will sharpen their persuasive-writing skills and help them develop a distinctive voice and writing style.

WHAT YOU'LL FIND IN THIS BOOK

Part I (Chapters 1-12) presents the writing strategies individually, with instructional notes and student exercises and reference sheets. Part II (Chapters 13-15) gives you tools to help students apply their practice to draft, revise, and edit their essays. Part III deals with problem-solving and assessment and includes student practice with scoring several essays against a rubric. Also in Part III are additional skill-sharpening games and activities for the whole class, some questions for close reading, a glossary of terms, a quiz on the terms, and 101 writing prompts. Together, this resource presents a metaphorical Swiss Army knife of writing strategies that you and your students can use to tackle any writing task with confidence.

In Part I (Chapters 1-12), each chapter begins with an explanation, followed by reproducible student activities and worksheets that provide definitions, examples, and practice. "Teaching Notes and Answers" at the end of each chapter provide you with instructional information, examples, and activity answers.

A Style Points Quiz with answers follows Chapter 12 as a culminating assessment activity. Use this assessment to guide instruction and assess understanding.

Part II (Chapters 13-15) focuses on helping your students apply their style-points practice to the essay-writing process. Chapter 13 includes a powerful pre-writing strategy, summaries of the major points, two student-revision strategies, and ways to help your students edit for coherence and organization.

Chapter 14 provides you with problem-solving and assessment information to pinpoint problems and to give your students practice scoring an essay against a provided six-point rubric. Finally, additional whole-class games and activities in Chapter 15 add even more effective spice to your instruction. The "Resource" section also provides you with 101 writing prompts and a glossary of key terms, along with a final quiz that tests their knowledge of the terms you've taught.

An important organizational note: After you assess the worksheets, return them to the students for reference. Students can keep them in a binder or portfolio. This allows them to track their progress, review past strategies, and return to past drafts for revision. It will be especially helpful as they bridge the transition from learning and practicing Part I writing strategies to applying those strategies in Part II essays.

HOW TO USE THE STYLE POINTS LESSONS IN YOUR CLASSROOM

Because the needs of teachers (and their students) vary so widely, this book is designed to give you as much flexibility as possible. Here are two basic approaches you might take.

Option 1: Go through the book's exercises in sequence. The student lessons in the first twelve chapters are cumulative: They progress from introductory exercises that introduce each strategy to short composition activities in which students apply each strategy in their own writing.

Each of the student worksheets contains some background definitions, examples, and explanations. But you will get the best instructional results if you introduce and teach the lesson first. The notes in the beginning of each chapter give you ideas of how to introduce and teach each concept that the students will work on.

Additionally, the "Teaching Notes and Answers" that follow each chapter provide you with specific instructional tips and information that applies to each exercise, as well as examples, definitions, and student-worksheet answers.

As you lead students through the lessons' concepts, focus on the examples and models provided to help you. Take time to read these aloud with students so they can see the strategies in action before they do their own writing.

Allow at least one class period (forty–fifty minutes) for each activity. Using this approach, the first part of the book will take at least twelve weeks to complete (more if you do every activity in each chapter).

Once students have completed Part I of the book, Part II will guide them through the process of applying the strategies by writing fully developed essays. The activities in Chapter 13 support students throughout the entire writing process: pre-writing, drafting, revising for coherence and organization, and self- and peer-revision.

For the first essay you assign, spend at least one class period on each activity to ensure that students are well-grounded in each stage of the writing process. This groundwork will pay off later, as it equips students with strategies they can use at each stage.

The whole-activities in Chapter 15 are designed to reinforce the strategies learned in Part I; these can be used at any time to practice and sharpen students' use of these strategies.

Option 2: Jump around based on the needs of your students. Each chapter in this book is self-contained so that you can use it individually out of sequence. If, for example, your students need work on verbs, use the activities in Chapter 3. For planning purposes, each activity is designed to take approximately one forty- to fifty-minute class period.

Chapter 14 provides a section on "Pinpointing Problems," which will help you identify specific strategies that you might teach based on past student-writing assessments.

Because no two teachers use any one book the same way, this book is designed so that you can flip back and forth between Part I and Part II based on your preferences and needs. The Chapter 15 activities are the one exception; these activities, which provide whole-class options for practicing and reinforcing skills, presume knowledge of the strategies from Chapters 1-12.

PART I

Style Points Persuasive Exercises for Student Practice

The twelve chapters that follow present an array of writing strategies. Each chapter begins with an explanation of the strategy, followed by reproducible student activities and worksheets that provide definitions, examples, explanations, and practice. "Teaching Notes and Answers" at the end of each chapter provide you with instructional information, examples, and activity answers.

At the end of Part I, you will find a Style Points Quiz that you can use to assess your students' understanding of the many strategies they will learn.

Ideas and Details— Build a Strong Structural Foundation

OVERVIEW

Nothing is more essential and central to a persuasive composition than the writer's main point. Chapters 1 and 2 provide students practice with developing the fundamental skills to construct a clear main point—a thesis—and develop specific, showing examples to support it.

Claims, reasons, and examples are the three "must-haves" of an excellent persuasive essay. First, the essay must clearly state its claim; second, it must tell why this claim is true and give reasons; and third, it must use examples and specific evidence to explain to and show the reader the validity of the claim and reasons.

Practicing with claims, premises, and examples gives students valuable experience in stating and developing their ideas clearly and cogently.

Begin instruction by doing the following exercise as a whole-class activity.

PRE- AND POST-POINTS ACTIVITY: TWO SIDES OF THE QUESTION

Before introducing students to the activities in Chapters 1 and 2, select one of the 101 topics from "Resources." Write the question on the board, and create two columns that explore both sides of the question, such as in the following example. Explain to students that this activity is an excellent pre-writing strategy for planning an essay. This is a strategy students can use to plan and write essays in Part II.

Question: Should gun control be further tightened?

PRO—YES	CON—NO
Reason and Example 1	Reason and Example 1
Reason and Example 2	Reason and Example 2
Reason and Example 3	Reason and Example 3

If students are having trouble, you can prompt them with the following examples.

Example: Pro

Large numbers of Americans die or are injured each year by gun violence. For example, each year 30,000 Americans die from guns. An additional 40,000 are injured in gun-related activities, costing our nation billions of dollars in medical and other expenses.

Example: Con

Law-abiding citizens should be able to have guns to protect themselves against criminals with guns. To demonstrate this fact, 99 percent of gun owners use them responsibly to protect themselves. During the Los Angeles riots of 1992, for example, many felt that their survival depended on their ability to protect themselves.

Ask students to share ideas until all six boxes are filled, supplying reasons and possible examples that address both sides of the question. If students are reluctant to look at both sides of the issue, explain that although an essay will make points on one side or the other, a strong essay will also address possible objections. Thinking about both sides of the question, therefore, will better prepare the writer to compose the most persuasive essay.

After completing the exercises in Chapters 1 and 2, try this exercise again. This will allow students to apply what they have learned, and you will be able to see how their understanding of reasons and examples has evolved.

CHAPTER 1

Claims and Premises— The Rhetorical Rod and Reel

KEY TERMS

Claim: The core of an argument, a statement of opinion that the writer supports with reasoning and evidence. Example – *Gun control should be further tightened.*

Premise: A reason that supports the validity of a claim. Example – *Gun control should be further tightened because guns do not deter crime.*

Thesis: A one-sentence statement of the writer's argument containing a claim and at least one premise. Example – *Gun control should be further tightened because guns do not deter crime.*

THE WHAT, WHY, AND HOW OF THE THESIS STATEMENT

The thesis is the most important sentence in an essay. It is the main point boiled down to one clear sentence.

Because the rest of the essay depends on the thesis, students need to know what it is before they begin writing a first draft of an essay. A well-crafted thesis will give them direction in writing their essays, help them organize their essays clearly, and most important, provide their readers with a clear roadmap.

There is nothing new about the thesis. The ancient Greeks, who invented logic, knew that any successful argument needed to appeal to the reader through logic and reason. As a result, Aristotle, who invented the thesis, called it the enthymeme: a two-part invention that did for the essay what the rod and reel did for fishing.

Here's a humorous list that illustrates the point.

Reasons that Duct Tape Is the Most Ingenious and Versatile Tool Ever Invented

1. *It's vital to national security. It was first used by the U.S. Army to create a watertight seal on ammunition boxes.*
2. *It's out of this world. NASA astronauts carry duct tape on moon missions. It played a part in saving the Apollo 13 mission, and it was used to repair a fender on the lunar rover on the Apollo 17 mission.*
3. *It's a fashion statement. Entire wardrobes have been created with duct tape: pants, belts, purses, wallets, hats, visors, ties, and even prom dresses.*

4. *It's a medical miracle. One medical study reported that duct tape was useful in the treatment of warts, and it can be used for first aid as a temporary suture to close up a wound.*
5. *It's kind to animals. Hunters sometimes tape it to the bottom of a hunting dog's feet where the terrain is rough and full of burrs. Bee keepers use it to seal their bee hives when transporting hives.*

Although this list is hardly serious, it does feature a logical structure that goes back to the innovative Aristotle. First, it provides the reader with a clear claim: "Duct tape is the most ingenious and versatile tool ever invented." It then follows the claim with five clear, specific premises (or reasons) that support the claim.

The logical structure that holds this list together is the same one that students need to give their essays a solid structural foundation. No matter what they are writing, students need a point—a well-formed thesis. Understanding the difference between a claim and a premise will help students construct a clear, logical point that will help both them and their readers.

Students may have experience writing a thesis with a supporting claim, but the important point of this chapter is that a single claim is not enough. A complete thesis must contain a claim and at least one premise. It provides the writer with a coherent plan of how to organize the essay, and it gives the reader a kind of sneak preview of where the essay is going.

For example, using the previous list, a writer might write a five-paragraph essay with the following thesis.

> **Claim:** *Duct tape is the most ingenious and versatile tool ever invented.*
> **Premise 1:** *It's vital to national security.*
> **Premise 2:** *It's a medical miracle.*
> **Premise 3:** *It's a fashion statement.*
>
> **Single-sentence thesis:** *Duct tape is the most ingenious and versatile tool ever invented because it's vital to national security, it's a medical miracle, and it's a fashion statement.*

Whether responding to an Advanced Placement argumentative prompt, an SAT essay prompt, or a state writing-assessment question, students can use the strategies explained in this chapter to construct a one-sentence thesis that will make their essay both cogent and credible—cogent because it will be structured based on sound logic and reason, and credible because it will reassure readers that they are in the hands of a writer who has purpose and direction.

The activities that follow will help students to understand both what a thesis is and also why it is so important to structure a thesis based on a clear claim and precise premises. Refer to "Teaching Notes and Answers" following the activities for specific instructional information and activity answers.

Chapter 1 Exercises

1. **Logic Meets Duct Tape.** Students do a close reading of a short passage, analyzing its structure to see how it holds together logically. Once students have read it carefully, they then imitate the structure by writing about a topic of their own. This is an excellent whole-class activity to illustrate the greatest variety of observations. The goal here is to help students see that even though the list is humorous, it has a logical structure based on sound reasoning.

2. **The Two Parts of a Thesis.** Explicit examples show students the difference between claims and premises.

3. **Thesis under Construction.** This activity provides students with questions and a two-step process for constructing a thesis with a claim and premises.

4. **The Claim Game.** Students use their own ideas to construct a solid thesis and argument. This game is also a fun and instructive whole-class activity.

5. **Build Your Ethos with Counterarguments.** Students learn why it is important to consider both sides of an argument.

6. **Television: Terrific or Terrible?** This activity presents students with a single focused question, the kind of question they will face on AP exams, SAT essays, and state writing assessments.

7. **Transitions: Transportation You Need.** Students increase the coherence of their writing by making sure their sentences and paragraphs flow smoothly from beginning to end.

8. **Not Your Average Writing Assignment.** This activity will demonstrate to students that writing isn't just about logic and reason; it also requires the writer to use imagination.

1. LOGIC MEETS DUCT TAPE

Read the following list carefully, focusing especially on how it is organized.

Reasons That Duct Tape Is the Most Ingenious and Versatile Tool Ever Invented

1. *It's vital to national security. It was first used by the U.S. Army to create a watertight seal on ammunition boxes.*
2. *It's out of this world. NASA astronauts carry duct tape on moon missions. It played a part in saving the Apollo 13 mission, and it was used to repair a fender on the lunar rover on the Apollo 17 mission.*
3. *It's a fashion statement. Entire wardrobes have been created with duct tape: pants, belts, purses, wallets, hats, visors, ties, and even prom dresses.*
4. *It's a medical miracle. One medical study reported that duct tape was useful in the treatment of warts, and it can be used for first aid as a temporary suture to close up a wound.*
5. *It's kind to animals. Hunters sometimes tape it to the bottom of a hunting dog's feet where the terrain is rough and full of burrs. Bee keepers use it to seal their bee hives when transporting hives.*

Directions

   I. List at least four things that you notice about the way the passage is organized.

      1. _____

      2. _____

      3. _____

      4. _____

   II. Using the duct-tape list as a model, write your own list of five about something you find praiseworthy. Make sure to include 1.) a title that states: "Reasons that ... "; 2.) numbered reasons written in complete sentences; and 3.) a few examples or details after each reason.

2. THE TWO PARTS OF A THESIS

The thesis—the main argument of an essay boiled down to one sentence—is made up of two essential parts: a single claim and at least one premise.

Let's examine a sample thesis:

Duct tape is the most ingenious and versatile tool ever invented because it's vital to national security, it's a medical miracle, and it's a fashion statement.

The claim is the core of the argument. It is what you want your reader to believe by the end of the essay. A claim is an opinion—not a fact. In the case of our sample thesis, the core of the argument is to persuade the reader that duct tape is the most ingenious and versatile tool ever invented.

A premise is a reason that you provide to support your claim. It answers the question "Why is this true?" or "Why should this be done?" In the case of our duct-tape thesis, we have three premises: 1.) It's vital to national security; 2.) It's a medical miracle; and 3.) It's a fashion statement.

The genius of a complete thesis with a claim and premises is that it fulfills the reader's need for a logical foundation as well as a logical roadmap of where the essay is going. With our duct-tape thesis, for example, the reader knows both what we are going to argue in our essay—the final destination so to speak—as well as the stops along the way, which are the premises of the argument.

Directions

I. Read the following thesis statements. Underline the premises and write down the number of premises in each thesis.

We should not ban human cloning research because it could bring about medical solutions for millions of people.

Because it may lead to future eugenics, we should ban human-cloning research.

Sports benefit your overall health because they relieve stress in your muscles, they work your cardiovascular system, and they provide your brain with needed oxygen.

That government is best which governs the least, because its people discipline themselves. —Thomas Jefferson

Gun control should be further tightened because guns do not deter crime.

Because gun control punishes only law-abiding citizens, it should not be further tightened.

II. Write your own thesis on a topic of your own choosing, including a single claim and at least three premises.

3. THESIS UNDER CONSTRUCTION

Constructing a thesis boils down to two key steps.

Step 1. State what your claim is (the claim, or the "what").

Step 2. Tell why your claim is valid (the premise, or the "why").

For example, if you were trying to persuade your parents to extend your curfew, you would begin by stating what your claim is:

My curfew should be extended by an hour.

The next step would be to tell your parents why your claim is valid. For example:

I have never violated my curfew.
I have never acted irresponsibly while out at night.
I have always called home to inform you of any changes in my evening plans.

Put together into a single sentence, your thesis contains one claim and three premises:

My curfew should be extended by one hour because I have never violated my curfew, I have never acted irresponsibly while out at night, and I have always called home to inform you of any changes in my evening plans.

Armed with a solid thesis, you now have a foundation for your essay. As the writer, you know where you are going. In addition, your reader has a clear idea of the road ahead. Now you are prepared to put the flesh on the bare bones of your argument.

Directions

I. Select one of the following questions.

1. Who is the most influential living person? What makes the person influential?
2. What are the qualities that make an effective leader? Why are these qualities so important?
3. How have computers impacted our society? Has the overall impact been positive or negative?
4. What is a product you would endorse? What makes it so great?
5. What is something you would say is overrated or underrated? Why?
6. What is a key quality to success in today's world? Why is this quality so important?
7. What specific change would you make to your community, nation, or world to improve life for everyone? Why would this change be effective?

II. Brainstorm at least eight possible answers on a separate piece of paper.

III. Once you have at least eight ideas, construct a thesis that contains a claim and at least three supporting premises.

4. THE CLAIM GAME

Directions

Use the following three steps to construct a brief argument.

I. "What?" State what your claim is. State a claim that you believe in strongly. It should be a complete sentence that states an opinion, such as:

> *Cell phones have improved our society.*
> *Parents should never limit their child's television viewing.*
> *Sports are essential for teaching young people life skills.*
> *Hermit crabs are the greatest pet any child could have.*
> *Bacon should be served with every meal.*
> *Homework is overrated.*

_____

II. "Why?" Tell why your claim is true. Defend your claim, giving at least one clear reason it is true.

_____

_____

III. Put your claim (the "what") together with your premise (the "why") into a single topic sentence, then write a paragraph defending your thesis.

_____

_____

_____

_____

_____

_____

_____

_____

_____

_____

Chapter 1 Claims and Premises—The Rhetorical Rod and Reel

5. BUILD YOUR ETHOS WITH COUNTERARGUMENTS

Good writers understand that their success relies on not alienating their readers. The Greeks called this *ethos*: the writer's ability to establish credibility with the reader. They knew that an audience was more easily persuaded if they felt that the writer had good sense, good will, and good character.

A writer builds credibility in a counterargument by anticipating and answering objections that a reader might have. To do this, the writer must look at both sides of an issue, instead of just the side that he or she is arguing. Writers who acknowledge the opposition are seen as more confident, more comprehensive, and more cogent by their readers because they are not afraid to take on opposing viewpoints. By anticipating and addressing the opposition, they reassure their readers that they have a broad perspective on the entire issue, instead of a narrow focus on only one side.

In the following examples, a writer is arguing against legalized gambling. Instead of focusing on just arguments for his point of view, he rebuts opposing viewpoints by including arguments that the other side might make.

> **[Opposing viewpoint]** *Although gambling provides some economic boost in jobs and tourism,* **[rebuttal]** *this boost is offset by the loss of profits and jobs it causes in small businesses that offer non-gambling pastimes.*

> **[Opposing viewpoint]** *Although some people argue that gambling increases tax revenues for a community,* **[rebuttal]** *the reality is that gambling actually decreases revenues because of the increased crime and bankruptcies that come to any community that adopts legal gambling.*

Directions

Imagine that you are writing on the topic of gun control, arguing that it should not be further tightened. Use the information in the following chart to write two counterarguments. First state a pro argument, and then refute that argument with a rebuttal from the con side.

Topic: Should gun control be further tightened?

PRO	CON
Large numbers of Americans die or are injured each year by gun violence.	Law-abiding citizens should be able to have guns to protect themselves against criminals with guns.
The 2nd Amendment applies to state militias, not an individual's right to bear arms.	The 2nd Amendment is rightly interpreted to guarantee the individual right to bear arms.

Counterargument 1:

_____

_____

_____

_____

Counterargument 2:

_____

_____

_____

_____

6. TELEVISION: TERRIFIC OR TERRIBLE?

Directions

What would you argue is the best thing or the worst thing on television? Write a brief editorial in which you argue for one thing that you think is either the best or the worst thing on television.

I. Brainstorm. Create a list of things on television that you would argue are either terrific or terrible.

Terrific   **Terrible**

_____   _____

_____   _____

_____   _____

_____   _____

_____   _____

II. State what your claim is. Select the single thing on television that you feel is either the most terrific or the most terrible and state a claim about it:

_____

III. Tell why your claim is true. Identify the single most powerful reason that your claim is true.

_____

_____

IV. Complete the argument. Put your claim and premise together in a single topic sentence, then write a paragraph defending your thesis.

7. TRANSITIONS: TRANSPORTATION YOU NEED

A writer must help a reader navigate from the beginning to the end of a composition. The reader should not become mired or stalled; instead, the trip from the hook to the conclusion should be smooth and seamless. Syntactical signposts, called transitions, show how ideas within a sentence relate logically to each other, and how the ideas in one sentence relate to those in the sentence that follows.

Directions

Read the following two versions of the paragraph. Which one is more coherent? In the more coherent version, what specific signal words does the writer use to guide the reader?

Version 1

July 20, 1969, is a pivotal date in the history of technological advancement. Neil Armstrong walked on the moon, an unparalleled human achievement that demonstrated the ability of technology to transport and liberate humankind from its limits. Back on Earth, a miraculous demonstration of technological advancement was the fact that Americans were able to sit in their living rooms and watch Armstrong take those first steps. Television made it possible for millions of Americans to be eyewitnesses to a milestone in the history of humanity, demonstrating its potential power to inform, inspire, and unite. Four decades after that first moonwalk, television's promise has fallen well short of its potential. It has deadened thought, and it has distracted and isolated people.

Version 2

July 20, 1969, is a pivotal date in the history of technological advancement. On that day, Neil Armstrong walked on the moon, an unparalleled human achievement that demonstrated the ability of technology to transport and liberate humankind from its limits. That same day back on Earth another miraculous demonstration of technological advancement was the fact that Americans were able to sit in their living rooms, watching and listening on television as Armstrong took those first steps. Television made it possible for millions of Americans to be eyewitnesses to a milestone in the history of humanity, demonstrating its potential power to inform, inspire, and unite. Four decades after that first moonwalk, however, television's promise has fallen well short of its potential. Instead of informing, it has become a distraction. Instead of inspiring, it has deadened thought. Instead of uniting, it has isolated people.

8. NOT YOUR AVERAGE WRITING ASSIGNMENT

Directions

Sometimes it is as important to come up with reasons not to do something as it is to come up with reasons to do something. It can also be a lot of fun and generate some laughter. Create a list of at least ten reasons *not* to do something. Begin with a title that states your claim, then number your reasons.

Use these ideas to come up with your own topic:

> *Ten reasons not to talk back to your mother.*
> *Ten reasons not to get your driver's license.*
> *Ten reasons not to buy a school lunch.*
> *Ten reasons not to chew gum.*
> *Ten reasons not to buy a new car.*
> *Ten reasons not to watch television.*
> *Ten reasons not to go bowling.*
> *Ten reasons not to take piano lessons.*
> *Ten reasons not to sing in public.*
> *Ten reasons not to do this assignment.*

Ten reasons not to _____

1. _____

2. _____

3. _____

4. _____

5. _____

6. _____

7. _____

8. _____

9. _____

10. _____

Chapter 1 Teaching Notes and Answers

1. LOGIC MEETS DUCT TAPE

This activity requires no set-up. Before students write on their own topics, however, make sure that you have pointed out the claim and the premises that hold the list together logically.

Samples of things that students should notice:

1. The title states the main point of the list.
2. Each item in the list begins with the same word.
3. Each item on the list follows the same pattern: a reason followed by details.
4. Each item on the list is a reason.
5. The list moves from general ideas to more specific ideas.
6. Each colon is followed by specific details that relate to the general reason stated.

When students create their own lists in part II of the assignment, use the three points in the directions as your major criteria for evaluation.

Good follow-up activity: Ask students to use the lists they create to write single-sentence thesis statements that incorporate a single claim and three premises.

2. THE TWO PARTS OF A THESIS

The instructions of the exercise explain the differences between a claim and premise and provide examples. If you do this exercise as a class activity, you could read the introductory part together before students begin work.

Teaching note: Point out that a premise does not necessarily have to follow a claim. As in #2 and #6, a thesis statement may open with a premise and finish with a claim.

Answers

In each answer, the premises are underlined followed by the total number of premises in parenthesis.

1. *We should not ban human cloning research <u>because it could bring about medical solutions to millions of people</u>. (1)*
2. *<u>Because it may lead to future eugenics</u>, we should ban human cloning research. (1)*
3. *Sports benefit your overall health <u>because they relieve stress in your muscles, they work your cardiovascular system, and they provide your brain with needed oxygen</u>. (3)*
4. *That government is best which governs the least, <u>because its people discipline themselves</u>.* —Thomas Jefferson *(1)*
5. *Gun control should be further tightened <u>because guns do not deter crime</u>. (1)*
6. *<u>Because gun control punishes only law-abiding citizens</u>, it should not be further tightened. (1)*

The following four thesis statements may be used for additional practice.

I went to the woods because I wished to live deliberately, to front only the essential facts of life, and see if I could not learn what it had to teach, and not, when I came to die, discover that I had not lived. —Henry David Thoreau *(1)*

Because owning a pet encourages responsibility, every child should have one. (1)

We choose to go to the moon in this decade and do the other things, not because they are easy, but because they are hard, because that goal will serve to organize and measure the best of our energies and skills, because that challenge is one that we are willing to accept. —John F. Kennedy *(3)*

I believe that man will not merely endure: He will prevail. He is immortal, not because he alone among creatures has an inexhaustible voice, but because he has a soul, a spirit capable of compassion and sacrifice and endurance. —William Faulkner *(1)*

3. THESIS UNDER CONSTRUCTION

It is important to have students brainstorm at least eight possible answers. This stretches their thinking and forces them to go beyond the first obvious answers that pop into their minds. Before students do these exercises alone, you might model one by doing a whole-class brainstorm. By first seeing the possibilities of generating many ideas as a class, students are more likely to then generate more ideas on their own.

Sample Response

The impact of computers has been primarily positive because:

> *Computers have saved money, by providing cheap ways for people and businesses to communicate and store information.*
>
> *Computers have provided more ways to communicate.*
>
> *Computers have saved people time.*
>
> *Computers have opened doors for education.*
>
> *Computers have provided easier access to a variety of media and entertainment sources.*
>
> *Computers have democratized publishing, allowing everyone to have a voice.*
>
> *Computers have increased literacy, providing more opportunities for people to read and to learn to read.*
>
> *Computers have increased communication across cultures.*

Thesis: The impact of computers has been primarily positive because they have opened doors for education, saved people time, and increased communication across cultures.

4. THE CLAIM GAME

Have a student state a claim. Then ask other students to state premises (reasons) to support or refute it.

You can also ask students to pick a number between 0 and 101, or choose from the "101 Writing Prompts" in the "Resources" section.

How the three steps might be followed to construct a paragraph:

I. "What?" State what your claim is. State a claim that you believe in strongly. It should be a complete sentence that states an opinion. For example: *Everyone should try juggling.*

II. "Why?" Tell why your claim is true. Defend your claim, giving at least one clear reason that it is true. For example: *Because it builds the brain.*

III. Put your claim (the "what") together with your premise (the "why") in a single topic sentence, then write a paragraph defending your thesis.

Everyone should try juggling because it builds the brain. German researchers completed a study that showed adults who practiced juggling for a period of three months showed increased gray matter; in contrast, adults who did not juggle in the study showed no increase in brain size. Many people associate juggling with clowns, but with practice and persistence anyone can learn to juggle and reap its mental benefits. In addition to the brain boost documented by German researchers, it's also great exercise, a great way to learn to focus on the matter at hand, and a great way to improve hand-eye coordination.

5. BUILD YOUR ETHOS WITH COUNTERARGUMENTS

Open this activity by asking students the following question: "If you are arguing a topic, why is it a good idea to look at both sides of the issue, rather than just the one side you are arguing?"

Students might mention that looking at both sides allows you to see the big picture and therefore better construct a persuasive argument. They might also mention that a writer who takes on the opposition is more credible.

Next, pass out the handout and guide students through the explanation of ethos and of counterarguments. With students, look at the following counterarguments example on gambling before asking them to write their own counterarguments about gun control.

The following are examples of counterarguments that students might write using the pro arguments and the rebuttals from the handout's chart.

It is true that large numbers of Americans die or are injured each year by gun violence. However, without guns more people may die because law-abiding citizens will be unable to protect themselves against criminals with guns.

Although some claim that the Second Amendment applies to state militias rather than individuals, the truth is that the Second Amendment guarantees the individual's right to bear arms.

6. TELEVISION: TERRIFIC OR TERRIBLE?

Because the most important element of this writing assignment is the thesis, make sure students have stated a clear claim and at least one premise. In the following sample paragraph, for example, the thesis is clearly stated ("The worst thing on television is the commercials") and is followed by a single premise ("because they interrupt the viewer's train of thought, discouraging concentration").

Sample Response

The worst thing on television is the commercials because they interrupt the viewer's train of thought, discouraging concentration. A child watching a movie on television, for example, might become immersed in a wonderful story, such as The Wizard of Oz. *Just as the child becomes engrossed in the imaginative world of Dorothy, however, she is jolted back to the harsh reality of a world that wants to sell her shampoo, breakfast cereal, and cold medicine. And these commercial interruptions don't just happen once or twice, they happen at least every fifteen minutes. No wonder even adults have a hard time focusing on anything for more than a few minutes; television's commercialism is designed to discourage concentration. Instead of enjoying a coherent narrative over the course of a one- or two-hour period, television shocks and jolts its viewers with a nonsensical array of incoherent messages and images. In a modern age that is already full of a constant deluge of distractions, who needs to submit themselves to more? Instead, turn off the TV and pick up a book so that you can enjoy a good story at your own pace.*

7. TRANSITIONS: TRANSPORTATION YOU NEED

After handing out the worksheet, read the opening paragraph that explains the writer's responsibility to write coherently. Students will read the two versions of the paragraph about television to determine which one is more coherent. After they have read the paragraphs, ask individual students which paragraph they thought was more coherent. Students should recognize that Version 2 has words that signal the transitions between sentences, making it the more coherent paragraph.

Next, pass out the handout titled "Signal Words: Three Techniques for Coherent Writing," found in Chapter 13. Tell students that this sheet identifies the three major categories of signal words writers use to keep their writing coherent. As you read through the explanation of each signal-word category, have students return to Version 2 and circle the specific examples where the writer uses that category of signal word.

Finally, tell students to keep the handout about signal words for future reference since you will expect them to use transitions in their future writing assignments.

The following is Version 2 with the transitions and other signal words underlined.

July 20, 1969, is a pivotal date in the history of technological advancement. <u>On that day</u> Neil Armstrong walked on the moon, an unparalleled human achievement that demonstrated the ability of technology to transport and liberate humankind from its limits. <u>That same day</u> back on Earth <u>another</u> miraculous demonstration of technological advancement was the fact that Americans were able to sit in their living rooms, watching and listening on television as Armstrong took his first steps. Television made it possible for millions of Americans to be eye-witnesses to a milestone in the history of humanity, demonstrating its potential power to inform, inspire, and unite. Four decades <u>after</u> that first moonwalk, <u>however</u>, television's promise has fallen well short of its potential. <u>Instead</u> of informing, it has become a distraction. <u>Instead</u> of inspiring, it has deadened thought. <u>Instead</u> of uniting, it has isolated people.

8. NOT YOUR AVERAGE WRITING ASSIGNMENT

This assignment is fun, and it also shows that a claim and a premise alone are not enough to make an argument. For example, the following sample list states that one reason not to get a cell phone is that "It's a waste of money." Having stated this as a premise, students should be aware that in an essay they will have to do more than just "tell." They will have to "show" what specifically is meant by "a waste of money." The chapters that follow will give them a number of strategies for "showing" their readers using specific evidence, pictures, and details.

Ten Reasons Not to Get a Cell Phone

1. *It's a waste of money.*
2. *It makes your life more complicated.*
3. *It makes you perpetually available.*
4. *It must be constantly recharged.*
5. *It makes you a public menace.*
6. *It makes driving unsafe for you and others on the road.*
7. *It makes you constantly distracted.*
8. *It makes you a slave to a one-sided contract.*
9. *It might be bad for your health. (The jury is still out.)*
10. *Cell phone accessories are expensive.*

CHAPTER 2

Examples—Tell and Show

Emergencies have always been necessary to progress. It was darkness which produced the lamp. It was fog that produced the compass. It was hunger that drove us to exploration. And it took a depression to teach us the real value of a job. —Victor Hugo

---

KEY TERMS

Anecdote: A brief story that illustrates a point.

Deduction: Reasoning by moving from the general to the specific.

Example: A specific detail that illustrates a generalization.

Generalization: An inference that can be supported with examples.

Induction: Reasoning by moving from the specific to the general.

THE WHAT, WHY, AND HOW OF EXAMPLES

Good writing strikes a balance between the abstract and the concrete, the general and the specific. You might, for example, show students the quotation from Victor Hugo. It begins with a general statement that *tells* the reader about the relationship between emergencies and progress: "Emergencies have always been necessary to progress." Hugo then follows the general statement with four specific examples that *show* his point in more specific terms. Good examples give the reader specific details that illustrate a writer's point or a writer's generalizations.

The effective writer must continually work to balance telling with showing. There is nothing wrong with generalizations; we make them every day, and they help us make sense of our world. Effective writing, however, supports generalizations with specific, concrete examples that illustrate and show the validity of each generalization.

Many jokes are based on generalizations followed by specific, showing details. For example, the following list is based on the single generalization: "Your substitute teacher might be a little odd if ... "

> *He has the same first and last name: "Good morning class. My name is Alexander Alexander."*

> *He begins class by playing a medley of Beatles songs on his accordion.*

> *He informs you that in his previous job he was a taste-tester for a dog-food company.*

> *He shouts, "I'm sick of your insane and insolent demands!!!" when you ask permission to sharpen your pencil.*

He begins taking attendance by saying, "Is Algebra I here? Algebra I?"

He restates all of his directions to the class in his own made-up language that he calls "Joe-Speak."

He requires that all questions be submitted in writing.

He requires that all answers be given in the form of a question.

He spells out every fifth word: "Tonight's homework is on P-A-G-E seven."

He dismisses class by making the entire class sing the "Marine Corps Hymn": "All together now: 'From the halls of Montezuma, to the shores of … .'"

Like good writing in general, humorous writing relies on the power of specific, detailed examples. Notice how each of the punch lines creates a specific picture. The idea of "an odd substitute teacher" in the abstract is not funny, but the specific details in the images *show* us what "odd" means by example.

The exercises in this chapter supply numerous examples of how great writers use examples to illustrate their points. The exercises and writing assignments show students how examples and anecdotes can enliven their writing and add style and voice to their writing. Refer to "Teaching Notes and Answers" at the end of the chapter for specific teaching information, examples, and answers.

Chapter 2 Exercises

9. **Two Important Words.** This activity helps students recognize the difference between telling and showing and provides practice in balancing abstract, general ideas with concrete, specific ones.

10. **Persuading with the Three Appeals: Logos, Pathos, and Ethos.** Students learn and practice recognizing the three major appeals of persuasion.

11. **Using Details to Persuade: Statistics, Dialogue, and Quotations.** Students learn three specific ways to apply logos, pathos, and ethos to persuasive writing.

12. **Organizing with Examples.** Students apply deductive and inductive organization to take advantage of the flexibility that using examples offers.

13. **Anecdotes: The Secret Is Out.** Anecdotes are a powerful way to include short vignettes as examples to illustrate general ideas.

14. **Inductive Hook and Full-circle Conclusion.** This activity gives students a useful strategy for opening and closing a paragraph or essay.

15. **What, Why, and How.** Students are taken through the three important steps of generating an argument that both tells and shows.

16. **Take the Inductive Challenge.** This writing assignment challenges students to think inductively by writing specific, detailed examples that reveal a single general point.

17. **Story Time.** Students write an anecdote that illustrates a single point.

18. **Signs of the Specific Kind.** This fun activity helps students see that specific examples provide detailed pictures for a reader.

9. TWO IMPORTANT WORDS

The two words "for example" are possibly the two most important words in a writer's lexicon. These two words remind writers to support the abstract with the concrete, to balance the general with the specific, and to not just *tell* the reader, but also *show* the reader with specific, detailed examples.

The following are other transitional expressions you can use to signal the reader that you are going to show rather than just tell:

for instance	*to demonstrate*
to illustrate	*an example of this is*
such as	*specifically*

Notice how each of the following sentences uses one of the previous signal expressions to connect the gap between a general, telling statement and specific, showing examples.

> *Americans love their dogs. For example, more than 80 percent of dog owners say that they would risk their life for their dog.*

> *Computers have come a long way. To illustrate, today's musical greeting card is more powerful than the world's most powerful computer was sixty years ago.*

> *Sometimes things that we hate to do can actually help us in the long run, such as doing our algebra homework, running the mile in gym class, or giving a speech in English class.*

Directions

Finish each of the following telling statements by providing your own showing examples. Include one of the previous expressions to signal your movement from the general to the specific.

1. *Life today is much more hectic than it was fifty years ago …*

   _____

2. *Technology has made communication today much more effective than it was fifty years ago …*

   _____

3. *Hard work and diligent effort are often much more valuable than relying solely on good luck …*

   _____

10. PERSUADING WITH THE THREE APPEALS: LOGOS, PATHOS, AND ETHOS

For the Greeks, writing and speaking persuasively were no small matters; for them persuasion was the foundation of the democracy they invented. Persuasion was also a major course of study, called rhetoric, in which students learned the art of combining the faculties of reason and imagination toward the goal of persuading an audience. Back then, rhetoric wasn't just about knowing how to read and how to write; it was about knowing how to lead. The Greeks understood that leaders must know how to communicate a message persuasively to a specific audience, balancing clarity, passion, and eloquence. They knew that what you said was important, but they also knew that how you said it was often just as important.

To persuade a reader, the writer must establish credibility with the audience and appeal to the reader's reason and imagination. The Greeks used three terms for these three vital appeals: logos, pathos, and ethos.

Logos is an appeal to the reader's logic and reason. An argument must have a clear point and be backed up with detailed evidence and clear explanations. It should be organized so that your reader can follow your train of thought easily. Ideas must be clearly structured to appeal to the reader's desire for order and clarity.

Pathos is an appeal to the reader's imagination and emotion. With pathos you establish a distinctive tone, or attitude, toward your subject and audience. By using imagery, figurative language, and specific word choice, you go beyond just *telling* your reader something. Pathos *shows* the reader what you mean and keeps the reader interested enough to keep reading.

Ethos is an appeal to character, that is, the writer's ability to establish trust with the audience. To be successful, the writer must demonstrate credibility. To be persuaded, the reader must have trust in the writer's good sense, good will, and good character.

Directions

Read the following three public service announcements that warn about the dangers of smoking. For each ad, identify which of the three appeals the writer is using to persuade the reader.

1. *The warning label on packages of cigarettes in Japan says, "Your Health May Suffer, So Take Care Not to Smoke Too Much." The warning label in France says, "Smoking May Cause a Slow and Painful Death." The principal use for nicotine other than in cigarettes is insecticide. Smokers call them "coffin nails" for a reason.*
2. *The Surgeon General first warned about the dangers of cigarettes in 1929. Still, today, more than five trillion cigarettes are smoked each year. A burning cigarette contains over 4,000 chemicals—more than forty of which are known carcinogens. More than five million people die each year from tobacco use. According to the World Health Organization, in the time it takes you to read this paragraph, one current or former smoker will have died.*
3. *Smoking kills. Who would know better than former Surgeon General C. Everett Koop? When asked his opinion on the number of deaths caused by smoking, he said, "That's like two jumbo jets crashing and everybody being killed every day." No one is buying tickets to fly on those jets, but you can bet that somewhere in the world today, someone is buying his or her first pack of cigarettes.*

11. USING DETAILS TO PERSUADE: STATISTICS, DIALOGUE, AND QUOTATIONS

Appeal to logos with statistics. There are many ways to appeal to your reader's logic and reason, including stating a clear point, backing it up with cogent evidence, and organizing it coherently. One specific way to establish your logos is by using statistics. Objective details like numbers show the reader the validity of your point in concrete terms. Don't overwhelm your reader with statistics, however. Instead, select the ones you think are the strongest and most memorable. Also, consider your reader, and state the statistic so that it provides the best, clearest picture possible. For example, instead of saying "25.3 percent of teenagers say they like broccoli," round off the number and say, "1 in 4" or "one-fourth."

Appeal to pathos with dialogue. Your readers have brains, but they also have hearts, so don't forget the kinds of details that appeal to your reader's imagination and emotions, such as imagery, figurative language, and specific word choice. One specific way to establish your pathos is by using dialogue. Your readers have a natural affinity for the sound of other human voices; after all we have been listening to each other talk a lot longer than we have been reading words on paper. Like adding an anecdote, dialogue creates human interest, so sprinkle a bit of authentic-sounding dialogue in your essay. It will give your facts a little bit of the punch that comes from fiction and real life.

Appeal to ethos with quotations. Like lawyers arguing before a jury, good writers know that they must establish credibility and maintain the trust of readers. They do this in many ways, such as making clear points, presenting details, showing evidence, and writing in a sincere, confident voice. Adding a quotation helps you borrow the prestige and authority of experts, using their words to support your case. Integrate them smoothly into your own writing by framing them. For example, James C. Humes, a speechwriter for two American presidents, said, "A quotation in the middle of a talk is like a baseball pitcher's change of pace. A quotation arrests the audience's attention. It wakes them up. It energizes them." Notice the lead-in phrase provides the name and the qualifications of the speaker and integrates the quote. Using a quotation in this way allows the reader to judge its credibility.

Directions

The following three passages come from an essay in which the writer argues that spelling is overrated. Identify which of the three appeals the writer uses in each passage.

1. *Napoleon Bonaparte, the great French emperor and military leader, did not rank spelling very high on his list of priorities, saying, "A man occupied with public or other important business cannot, and need not, attend to spelling."*
2. *People waste too much time worrying about spelling. For example, as I'm writing this essay, instead of thinking carefully about my ideas, I'm wasting time thinking about things like, "How do you spell 'carefully' again? Is it with or without an 'e'?"*
3. *Even* The New York Times *has trouble with spelling. Since the year 2000, America's newspaper of record has misspelled the word "misspelled" fourteen times.*

12. ORGANIZING WITH EXAMPLES

To understand the full effect of examples in writing, you need to know the difference between deductive reasoning and inductive reasoning.

Deductive reasoning: moving from the general to the specific. Aspiring writers can learn a lot by studying how other writers balance the general and the specific. The following quote is deductive, that is, it begins with a general idea followed by specific, detailed examples. In other words, it first tells the reader, then shows the reader with examples and details. For example:

> *It is possible to own too much. A man with one watch knows what time it is; a man with two watches is never quite sure.* —Lee Segall

Segall begins with a general statement of opinion about owning too much. He then follows with a specific showing example explaining the generalization in concrete terms.

Inductive reasoning: moving from the specific to the general. Sometimes writers use inductive organization by beginning with specific details and examples that lead to a logical claim. Notice how the following quote by Kathy Seligman follows the inductive pattern by giving two specific examples—one from baseball and one from fishing—that lead to a logical general claim about achieving your goals.

> *You can't hit a home run unless you step up to the plate. You can't catch fish unless you put your line in the water. You can't reach your goals if you don't try.*

Directions

Analyze the following quotations and label them as deductive or inductive.

1. *Yes, there is Nirvana; it is in leading your sheep to a green pasture, and in putting your child to sleep, and in writing the last line of your poem.* —Kahlil Gibran
2. *Positive thinking is the key to success in business, education, pro football, anything that you can mention ... I go out there thinking that I'm going to complete every pass.* —Ron Jaworski
3. *To laugh often and much; to win the respect of intelligent people and the affection of children; to earn the appreciation of honest critics and endure the betrayal of false friends; to appreciate beauty; to find the best in others; to leave the world a bit better ... to know even one life has breathed easier because you lived. This is to be successful.* —Ralph W. Emerson
4. *In preparing a speech, remember to make brief notes; Abraham Lincoln wrote the "Gettysburg Address" on the back of an envelope.* —Unknown
5. *No horse gets anywhere until he is harnessed. No steam or gas ever drives anything until it is confined. No Niagara is ever turned into light and power until it is tunneled. No life ever grows great until it is focused, dedicated, disciplined.* —Harry Emerson Fosdick

13. ANECDOTES: THE SECRET IS OUT!

The word *anecdote* comes originally from Greek, meaning "things not given out." Today, however, good writers know that using anecdotes—brief stories that illustrate a point—is one of the best ways to support a point.

Specific stories about specific people are a powerful way to illustrate general truths and to keep the reader's attention. Brain research, for example, reveals that when given a variety of different types of material to read, people will always rate stories the highest for keeping their interest. Cognitive scientist Daniel T. Willingham reports that our brains seem predisposed to understanding and remembering stories, that stories "are treated differently in memory than other types of material."

Like examples, anecdotes show the reader your point. The key, therefore, is not just telling a story; rather, the stories you select must be relevant to your point. The stories you draw from don't have to be just about famous people. You can use stories of your personal experience, stories that you have heard from other ordinary people, or even stories you have discovered in fictional stories.

Directions

Read the following three anecdotes, and match each anecdote with the appropriate general statement that follows.

1. *At the Battle of Thermopylae in 480 B.C. the Greek forces faced an invading Persian army. Greatly outnumbered by the Persian forces, one of the Greek soldiers reported to the Spartan warrior Dieneces that the invading force had so many archers that their arrows would blot out the sun. Undaunted even by the overwhelming odds against him, Dieneces replied, "So much the better, we shall fight in the shade."*

2. *One day a friend of Socrates observed the great philosopher carefully studying some flashy items on display in the marketplace. Knowing Socrates' reputation for frugality, the friend asked, "Why, Socrates, do you come to the market, since you never buy anything?" Socrates responded, "I'm always amazed to see that there are so many things I can do without."*

3. *Two women came before King Solomon claiming to be the mother of a single baby boy. After briefly contemplating how to resolve the dispute, the king ordered his officers to bring him a sword. He then announced to the women that he would cut the child in two and give each woman a half. One of the women immediately cried out, saying, "Give her the living child rather than kill it!" while the other woman demanded, "Let it be neither mine or thine, but divide it." Solomon, recognizing that the compassion of the first woman identified her as the true mother, ordered that the baby be given to her.*

A. Knowledge of human psychology can come in handy when trying to solve complex problems. Anecdote # _____

B. Vain pursuit of material possessions brings little satisfaction. Anecdote # _____

C. Humor in the face of a stressful situation can dispel fear. Anecdote # _____

14. INDUCTIVE HOOK AND FULL-CIRCLE CONCLUSION

Examples are incredibly useful for helping you prove your point in the body of your essay. Examples and anecdotes also are excellent for hooking your reader's interest from the very beginning of your essay. Similarly, returning to an opening example or anecdote at the end of your composition will bring your reader full circle to a pleasing conclusion.

An inductive hook. Make a strong first impression on your reader by beginning with a specific example or anecdote that relates directly to your main point. Starting with a specific example or an anecdote will hook the reader's interest by providing concrete images of real people, places, and things. After your opening example or anecdote, you can then lead your reader from the specific to the general by stating your thesis. Using an inductive hook also opens the door for ending your composition with a smooth, satisfying conclusion.

A full-circle conclusion. When you are wrapping up your essay, return to your opening example or anecdote to give your reader the pleasing sense of coming full circle. Returning to the starting point will give the reader the satisfying, almost subliminal, feeling of completing a journey successfully.

Directions

Read the following passage on train travel. As you read, notice how the writer employs both an inductive hook and a full-circle conclusion.

> *Sitting in a train traveling from Manchester to London in 1990, a young woman got a billion-dollar idea. She began to imagine a character—"a bespectacled boy who did not know he was a wizard." Where else but in the friendly and comfortable confines of a train might someone like J.K. Rowling be inspired to write stories of the young wizard named Harry Potter?*
>
> *Beyond just literary inspiration, there are plenty of other reasons to be inspired by train travel. It's economical—typically half the cost of traveling by plane. It's flexible and hassle-free—no need to stand in long security lines or even make advanced reservations. And it's convenient—unlike airports, most train stations are located in the heart of the city, in easy walking distance from hotels, sightseeing, and shopping. Not only is train travel cheaper than airfare, it is also more consistently and reliably priced without the arbitrary constraints of airline pricing where, for example, a one-way ticket costs more than a round-trip ticket. In addition to economical sense, train travel also makes eco-sense since trains are more energy efficient, using 70 percent less energy and emitting up to 85 percent less air pollution than airplanes. But perhaps the best argument for train travel is the charm and relaxation of this most humane form of transportation. There's plenty of legroom, plenty of opportunities to move or walk around, and plenty of things to see right outside your window: wild life, rivers, mountains, small towns, and great cities. You'll have time to breath, relax, and imagine.*
>
> *J.K. Rowling may have imagined a young wizard flying on a broomstick, but she didn't get the idea in the cramped, claustrophobic seat of a flying jet airliner. Harry Potter was born on a train.*

1. What example or anecdote does the writer use to open the paragraph?
2. How does the concluding sentence bring the reader full circle?
3. As a reader, how would you describe the effect of the writer's use of an inductive hook and a full-circle conclusion?
4. Now select your own topic from the list of prompts your teacher gives you. Write an introductory paragraph using an inductive hook.

_____

_____

_____

_____

_____

_____

_____

_____

_____

_____

_____

_____

_____

_____

_____

15. WHAT, WHY, AND HOW

Directions

Use the following three steps to construct a brief argument.

I. State your claim. Select one of the following six questions and answer it with a claim that states your position.

1. What one thing would you say is overrated? Why?
2. What is the single best or worst change in life that has been brought about by technology in the past twenty-five years? Explain why it has specifically made life better or worse.
3. What one person would you say has contributed to making the world a better place? What has this person done specifically to deserve praise?
4. Was the life of the average individual more simple fifty years ago or is it simpler today?
5. Is having a pet an important part of growing up? Why or why not?
6. What is a place that you have visited that you think everyone should visit? Persuade your reader to go there.

II. Use a premise to tell why your claim is true. Defend your claim by listing at least four reasons it is true.

_____

_____

_____

_____

III. Use evidence and explanation to show how your thesis is true. Use detailed, concrete examples that show your reader that your thesis is valid.

_____

_____

_____

_____

IV. Compose. Combine your claims (What?), your best single premise (Why?), and your examples (How?) into a single paragraph that defends your thesis.

16. TAKE THE INDUCTIVE CHALLENGE

Directions

Write a paragraph in which you support a generalization with specific examples.

I. Select one of the following generalizations.

> *Cats/dogs are excellent/terrible pets.*
> *My hometown is an exciting/boring place to live.*
> *Owning a cell phone is a nuisance/a vital tool.*
> *Monday is the worst/best day of the week.*
> *The effect of technology on our lives is generally negative/positive.*
> *Advertising is a positive/negative aspect of modern life.*

II. List at least four specific, detailed examples that show your generalization is valid. For example, if you selected the generalization "My hometown is a boring place to live," you might write the following example: "Even in the middle of the day, the streets are empty, and the only people you see are young people wandering the sidewalks, looking for something to do."

    Example 1: _____

    Example 2: _____

    Example 3: _____

    Example 4: _____

III. Without reading your generalization, read your examples aloud to someone. See if they can determine what your generalization is by listening just to your examples.

IV. Revise your examples as necessary, and write a paragraph that is organized inductively, moving from your specific examples to your general point.

17. STORY TIME

Directions

Write an anecdote (a brief, true story) that illustrates a specific point or important idea. Whether you write a personal anecdote or an anecdote about a person from history or literature, the key consideration is to make sure that the anecdote illustrates a specific claim or generalization. In other words, your story needs to have a point. A natural way to organize an anecdote is inductively, moving from the specific details of the story to the general claim or generalization.

Read the following anecdote carefully. Then, identify which of the claims/generalizations that follows it best sums up its main point:

> A Tibetan Lama was speaking with a group of young monks. To make a point, he pulled out a large jar, set in on the table in front of him, and began placing fist-sized rocks in the jar one by one. When no more rocks would fit in the jar, he asked, "Is this jar full? Everyone replied: "Yes." He then reached under the table and pulled out a bucket of gravel. He dumped some of the gravel in the jar and shook it gently as the gravel worked its way between the rocks. He then asked, "Is this jar full?" The monks began to catch on, saying, "Probably not." The Lama then reached down and pulled out a bucket of sand. He dumped some of the sand into the jar and shook it gently as the sand worked its way between the rocks and the gravel. He then asked, "What is the point of this demonstration?" One young monk responded, "The point is, no matter how full your day, you can always fit some more things in." The Lama responded sternly: "No, the point is that if you don't put the big rocks in first, you'll never get them in at all."

The following are some examples of specific claims and generalizations that might be illustrated using an anecdote.

> The most important quality of a successful person is the desire to make his/her own breaks.

> Human beings have the ability to rationalize virtually any behavior.

> Even one word misunderstood can create a lot of problems.

> Creative thinking is more important than logical thinking.

> To live a less chaotic life, we need to set priorities.

> Students can always come up with an excuse for not doing homework.

> Just because someone has a disability doesn't mean he/she can't achieve great things.

> We can learn just as much from our failures as from our successes.

> Some of the best things in life cost very little.

Using one of the previous claims, or one of your own, write a paragraph that includes at least one specific anecdote.

_____

_____

_____

_____

_____

_____

_____

_____

_____

_____

_____

_____

_____

_____

_____

_____

_____

_____

_____

_____

18. SIGNS OF THE SPECIFIC KIND

It's easy to make generalizations, but good writers know how to back them up with specific details and examples.

Directions

Create a title that begins with the words *Signs That*. Use the title to state a general idea, such as *Signs That You Are a Harry Potter Fanatic*. Then come up with at least ten specific examples that illustrate the generalization in concrete, specific terms. For example, notice how the following list supports the generalization in its title with ten specific, detailed examples.

Signs That Your Substitute Teacher Might Be a Little Odd

He has the same first and last name: "Good morning class. My name is Alexander Alexander."

He begins class by playing a medley of Beatles songs on his accordion.

He informs you that in his previous job he was a taste-tester for a dog food company.

He shouts, "I'm sick of your insane and insolent demands!!!" when you ask permission to sharpen your pencil.

He begins taking attendance by saying, "Is Algebra I here? Algebra I?"

He restates all of his directions to the class in his own made-up language that he calls "Joe-Speak."

He requires that all questions be submitted in writing.

He requires that all answers be given in the form of a question.

He spells out every fifth word: "Tonight's homework is on P-A-G-E seven."

He dismisses class by making the entire class sing the "Marine Corps Hymn": "All together now: 'From the halls of Montezuma, to the shores of... .'"

Use one of the following ideas, or come up with your own.

Signs that you are in trouble with your parents
Signs that you are bored
Signs that you are a soccer player
Signs that your teacher is in a bad mood
Signs that you are a bad driver
Signs that you are not doing well in your math class
Signs that you have not been getting enough sleep lately
Signs that a celebrity is overexposed in the media
Signs that you spend too much time online
Signs that you have been drinking too much caffeine

Chapter 2 Teaching Notes and Answers

9. TWO IMPORTANT WORDS

Before presenting this activity, you might show students the list titled "Signs That Your Substitute Teacher Might Be a Little Odd." Have students look at the list and discuss the following question: "How does the writer of this list go beyond just telling the reader his point and show the reader what is meant by 'odd'?" Discussion of this question will reinforce the important role examples play in creating specific, detailed pictures for the reader.

Possible Answers

Life today is much more hectic than it was fifty years ago. For example, today the average person works more than forty hours per week and takes less vacation than a worker did fifty years ago.

Technology has made communication today much more effective than it was fifty years ago. For instance, the cell phone has allowed us to be in contact with just about anyone no matter where we, or they, are in the world.

Hard work and diligent effort are often much more valuable than relying solely on good luck. For example, a person who has worked to earn a four-year degree has a much better chance of landing a well-paying job than someone without a degree.

10. PERSUADING WITH THE THREE APPEALS: LOGOS, PATHOS, AND ETHOS

This activity introduces three important persuasive appeals that date back to ancient Greece. Before passing out the handout, tell students the following: "I am going to read you three anti-smoking public-service announcements. I want you to listen carefully to each to decide which one you think is the most persuasive. Be prepared to explain your choice." Then, read the PSAs aloud as students listen. Next, call on individual students to get their reactions. Explain to students that persuasive writers know some very old tricks that help them form effective arguments. Pass out the handout, and take students through a discussion of rhetoric and the explanation of the three appeals.

Next, have students read through the three anti-smoking appeals again. This time their mission is to match up each of the appeals with appropriate PSA. Don't worry about whether students get the exact "right" answers here; the major goal here is to help students become familiar with the basic elements of each appeal.

You might follow up this activity with a project in which students design their own advertisement for a product, using one or more of the appeals. Plan to have them present their ads to the class to further discuss the different uses of appeals in the ads. Also, keep your eyes open for a television, radio, or magazine ad that you might share with students to further discuss the appeals. Using ads with pictures will help expand their knowledge of persuasion beyond just the "written" word.

Answers

1. *Pathos*
2. *Logos*
3. *Ethos*

11. USING DETAILS TO PERSUADE: STATISTICS, DIALOGUE, AND QUOTATIONS

Begin this activity by writing the following quotation on the board. Ask students if it is an effective description of the three appeals and why it is or isn't.

> *Logos, ethos, and pathos appeal to the brain, gut, and heart of your audience. While our brain tries to sort the facts, our gut tells us whether we can trust the other person, and our heart makes us want to do something about it.*
> —Jay Heinrichs

After discussion of the quotation, let students know that today you will be talking about using the three appeals along with different types of details to persuade.

Next, pass out the handout, and, as a class, read through the three descriptions, reviewing the definitions of logos, pathos, and ethos, and introduce the three types of details (quotations, dialogue, and statistics). Then read the directions and the three essay excerpts. Ask students to make their case for which appeal goes best with each excerpt. The key here is not exact "right" answers; you want to get students talking about the way the writing in the excerpts relates to the appeals and the different types of details.

After this activity, consider selecting one of the topics from "101 Writing Prompts" and having students brainstorm possible ways they might argue the question using the three different appeals along with the three types of details. Have students do this in pairs or small groups, or conduct it as a whole-class activity to get everyone's input.

Answers

1. *Ethos—Quotation*
2. *Pathos—Dialogue*
3. *Logos—Statistics*

12. ORGANIZING WITH EXAMPLES

Although this activity provides an explanation and examples that show the difference between deductive and inductive organization, you might introduce the lesson with the following two quotations and ask which makes the most effective point.

> *Emergencies have always been necessary to progress. It was darkness that produced the lamp. It was fog that produced the compass. It was hunger that drove us to exploration. And it took a depression to teach us the real value of a job.*

> *It was darkness that produced the lamp. It was fog that produced the compass. It was hunger that drove us to exploration. And it took a depression to teach us the real value of a job. Emergencies have always been necessary to progress.*

Discussing the two quotes will help students see the differences between moving from the general to the specific (deductive) and moving from the specific to the general (inductive). Both quotes are effective; however, since Victor Hugo chose to use deductive organization in the first quote, we can at least say that he thought the point was more effectively made using deductive organization.

Answers

1. *Deductive*
2. *Deductive*
3. *Inductive*
4. *Deductive*
5. *Inductive*

The following are additional quotations you can use to reinforce the difference between deductive and inductive organization.

Inductive
Look at a stone cutter hammering away at his rock, perhaps a hundred times without as much as a crack showing in it. Yet at the hundred-and-first blow it will split in two, and I know it was not the last blow that did it, but all that had gone before. —Jacob A. Riis

Deductive
Use what talents you have; the woods would have little music if no birds sang their song except those who sang best. —Reverend Oliver G. Wilson

Deductive
Having the world's best idea will do you no good unless you act on it. People who want milk shouldn't sit on a stool in the middle of a field in hopes that a cow will back up to them. —Curtis Grant

Deductive
Perseverance is a great element of success. If you only knock long enough and loud enough at the gate, you are sure to wake up somebody.
—Henry Wadsworth Longfellow

Inductive
I don't recruit players who are nasty to their parents. I look for players who realize the world doesn't revolve around them. —Pete Carill

13. ANECDOTES: THE SECRET IS OUT!

This activity introduces the anecdote as a way to use narrative examples in an essay. Before doing the activity, you might use the following anecdote about the word "anecdote" to provide some background for students:

The word anecdote comes originally from Greek and means "things not given out." Ancient historians were encouraged to write glowing histories of their patrons, leaving out any details that, although true, might portray their subjects in something other than a positive light. The sixth-century historian Procopius, for example, wrote an uncomplimentary account of the life of Byzantine Emperor Justinian, which he titled Anecdota ("secret history"). Characteristic of this past era, Procopius's book went unpublished in his lifetime, and—thankfully for him—it did not surface until long after his death.

Emphasize that anecdotes are stories about specific people in specific places. Students may use a personal anecdote based on their own experiences, or about other people, such as friends, people in the news, historical figures, or fictional characters. The key, however, is that the anecdote is relevant to the composition's main point.

As a follow-up activity, you might have students collect anecdotes from articles in newspapers and news magazines. This illustrates that professional writers know the power of personal stories to keep a reader's interest. As students share their collected anecdotes, have them discuss how the anecdote helped to illustrate the key points that the writer was trying to make.

Answers

A. 3
B. 2
C. 1

14. INDUCTIVE HOOK AND FULL-CIRCLE CONCLUSION

Because this concept can be challenging, the following activity sets up students for success. First, read the following four examples. Then ask students to listen carefully to determine what single generalization they can make for each of the examples. Once you have read the examples, give students a moment to think and write down their generalizations. Then call on students to share answers. Student answers should be close to the following generalization: *Some of science's most innovative technologies are derived from studying nature.*

Example 1
Scientists, searching for a surface that would be resistant to germs and bacteria, have turned to the shark. Noticing that sharks don't collect algae or barnacles on their bodies like other sea creatures do, scientists analyzed the shark's skin and discovered a coat of microscopic bumpy scales that are not only resistant to algae and barnacles, but are also resistant to harmful bacteria. They have used the shark's skin as a model for designing a germ- and bacteria-repellant plastic wrap that can be used in hospitals to reduce contamination of frequently touched surfaces, such as light switches and handles.

Example 2
When Swiss inventor George de Mestral returned with his dog from a walk, he noticed that he and his dog were covered with cockleburrs. Instead of being annoyed, he studied the burrs under a microscope where he noted their hook-like shape. Engineering artificial fasteners that replicated the ones he found in nature took a few years, but Mestral was eventually successful in creating his easy-to-use hook and loop fastener. He registered his invention in 1958. For the name of his product, he blended two French terms: "vel" from velvet and "cro" from crochet (little hook).

Example 3
Japanese engineers designed the front of their bullet train using the bill of the kingfisher as a model. Noticing that the birds barely make a ripple on the water when they dive through the air and into the water for fish, engineers developed a beak-like nose that made the trains 10 percent faster and 15 percent more fuel efficient.

Example 4

British scientists have developed a revolutionary new technology for the blind by studying echolocation, the sensory system that allows bats to "see" in the dark. The Ultracane emits ultrasonic pulses that cause the cane's handle to vibrate when objects are nearby. Because the feedback provided by the cane is silent, the blind are freed to hear the sounds of their environment.

Once students have written their own examples, make sure to provide time to complete the "challenge" portion of the assignment with one or more partners. This will provide them with necessary feedback for revising their paragraphs.

Possible Answers

1. The writer uses an anecdote about J.K. Rowling.
2. The concluding sentence refers to Harry Potter, the subject of the opening anecdote.
3. The story is an interesting one, keeping the reader engaged from beginning to end. Since the paragraph is grounded in the train-related Rowling/Potter anecdote in the beginning, the reference to Potter at the end brings the reader full circle.
4. Now select your own topic from the list of prompts your teacher gives you. Write an introductory paragraph using an inductive hook.

For more topics, see "101 Writing Prompts" in the "Resources" section.

15. WHAT, WHY, AND HOW

After introducing and reading through the three questions on the worksheet, you might show or read students the following model paragraph. Ask them to identify where the writer provides the what, the why, and the how:

> [What] *Wikipedia is one of the best reference tools available* [Why] *because it is the most comprehensive and up-to-date reference source you will ever find. Wikipedia is simply the largest single compilation of knowledge in the history of the human race. It dwarfs all other sources.* [How] *For example, compared to* The Encyclopedia Britannica's *65,000 articles, Wikipedia features nearly 3,000,000 articles, and that number is growing, literally by the minute. The reason we can say "literally by the minute" is because the content on Wikipedia is constantly being updated, added to, and edited. If, for example, a celebrity dies today, chances are you'll find it reflected in that celebrity's online Wikipedia biography today! Less than two weeks after Michael Jackson's death, for example, Wikipedia featured not just a biography of Michael Jackson, but also a specific article on "The Death of Michael Jackson." This article featured more than twenty sections and 129 footnotes. There are certainly other places to find information, but nowhere will you find so much in so little time.*

As students draft their own paragraphs, they can label the "what," "why," and "how" portions. Have student exchange papers for peer review and give each other feedback on how well each question is answered in the paragraph. Students can then use this feedback to revise their paragraphs.

16. TAKE THE INDUCTIVE CHALLENGE

Before students write their own paragraphs, read the example provided on the worksheet together. Then ask students to look at the list of nine generalizations that follows the example to determine which one best sums up the main point of the anecdote.

Students should be able to determine that it is "To live a less chaotic life, we need to set priorities." At this point you might explain that when writers use inductive organization, they don't always state their point explicitly; in fact, if the writer does a good job providing evidence and details, the point should be implicit enough that any reader will get the point.

After students write their own paragraphs, you might ask them to leave out the explicit point as they read their drafts to a partner to see if the partner can deduce the point based on the anecdote. The closer the partner gets to the point, the more effective the draft. Students can then use this feedback to polish their drafts.

Include time for some students to share their paragraphs with the entire class.

17. STORY TIME

Make sure that students include an explicit generalization at the end of the paragraph they write. That way, you can make sure they are making the connection between using a specific anecdote to illustrate a claim/generalization.

18. SIGNS OF THE SPECIFIC KIND

See the example on the worksheet called "Signs That Your Substitute Teacher Might Be a Little Odd." Use this list as your model.

Before students complete the activity, make sure that they read the model. Also, before students create their own "signs" list, select one of the topics and do a whole-class brainstorming activity. Students can also work in small groups to create their own lists on butcher paper to post for the class.

STRATEGY #2

Diction and Tone— Choose Words That Support the Thesis

OVERVIEW

Students understand that the clothes a person wears often reflect that person's personality. Similarly, it is the specific selection of words that distinguishes a writer's unique voice. Over and over, teachers report that a strong, distinctive voice is an essential ingredient in effective student writing.

Like the selection of fashions, the selection of vivid verbs and concrete nouns is one of the most powerful ways for students to give their essays a sense of unique voice. Proficient writers understand that words range from abstract to concrete and from general to specific; they also understand that in addition to telling, they must do a lot of showing, using specific, concrete language to paint pictures for the reader.

Equipped with the knowledge and skill of using specific, concrete word choices, students will be prepared to write essays in Part II of this book, essays that will be distinguished by the kind of powerful, specific word choices that characterizes great writing.

PRE- AND POST-POINTS ACTIVITY: TONE TIME

Before introducing students to the activities that follow for this strategy, select one of the topics from "101 Writing Prompts" found in the "Resources" section at the end of this book. Then write the question on the board.

Write the following ten adjectives on individual slips of paper, and hand out enough so that each student has a single adjective: *humorous, bitter, greedy, alarmist, moral, cautionary, authoritative, conversational, celebratory, optimistic.*

Tell students to imagine that the adjective they have been given reflects their attitude about the assigned question. Discuss the meaning of the adjectives if necessary. The students should write at least one complete sentence that reflects their assigned attitude without using the word itself.

If students struggle to do this, show them the following examples, and see if they can match up a separate tone word with each sentence.

Examples

Question: *Is the pursuit of money a virtue or a vice? Explain.*

Tone: Bitter
Money is the root of all evil. Nevertheless, we spend our futile lives vainly grasping for the branches of the money tree that are just out of reach.

Tone: Greedy
I don't know if the pursuit of money is a virtue or a vice, but the one thing I do know is that I never have enough, and I'm always looking for ways to get more. I crave cash, desire dollars, and covet currency.

Tone: Celebratory
Money is life's reward. It's what lifts us from the scummy streets to the palatial penthouses of the world.

After completing Activities 19–25, do this activity again. Point out to students that the adjectives they have been given reflect tone, the writer's attitude toward his/her subject or audience. They should notice that the more specific and concrete their diction (i.e., their word choice), the more individual their voices. By establishing a specific tone—an attitude—toward their topic or audience, it is almost impossible to write something that is not interesting. In contrast, without investing some emotion in the topic, writing becomes lifeless and dull.

To demonstrate the distinction between tone and diction, look at the sentence above with the "bitter" tone toward money. Because the writer wants to reflect a negative attitude, or tone, toward the subject, he selects words that have negative associations, such as "evil," "futile," "vainly," and "grasping." The negative diction (or word choice), therefore, results in a negative tone.

Similarly, the writer who adopts a "celebratory" tone toward money selects words with positive associations, such as "reward," "lifts," and "palatial penthouses." The writer's diction (word choice) is positive.

CHAPTER 3

Vivid Verbs—Video and Volume

> **KEY TERMS**
>
> **Action Verb:** A verb that describes specific action, evoking a picture, a sound, a smell, a taste, or a feeling, such as *scribble*, *scramble*, *weave*, *crash*, or *whistle*.
>
> **Active Voice:** A sentence in which the subject is the doer of the action, such as *Bill broke the window.*
>
> **Passive Voice:** A sentence in which the subject receives the action, such as *The window was broken by Bill.*
>
> **State-of-Being Verb:** A verb such as *is, am, was, were, being.*
>
> **Video Verb:** An action verb that provides pictures for the reader, such as *scramble*, *crush*, *weave*, or *snatch.*
>
> **Volume Verb:** An action verb that provides a soundtrack for the reader, such as *crash*, *gulp*, *whistle*, or *splash.*
>
> **Zeugma:** A figure of speech in which a single verb is used in two completely different ways. For example: *As his relationship with the girl continued, he fell madly in love and deeper in debt.*

THE WHAT, WHY, AND HOW OF VIVID VERBS

The cars hit.
The cars bumped.
The cars collided.
The cars smashed.

In an experiment conducted in 1974, subjects were shown a film of a traffic accident, and then asked questions about the accident. Some of the subjects were asked: "About how fast were the cars going when they hit each other?" Others were asked, "About how fast were the cars going when they smashed into each other?" The subjects who were asked the second question (*smashed*), gave a much higher estimated speed than the subjects who were asked the first question (*hit*).

When the subjects were brought back to the laboratory a week later and shown the film again, they were asked if they had seen any broken glass. In reality, there was no broken glass in the film, but several of the subjects reported seeing glass. Of those who were asked a week earlier how fast the cars were going when they *hit* each other, 14 percent said they saw glass; of those who were asked how fast the cars were going when they *smashed* into each other, 32 percent said they saw glass.

This experiment merely confirms what the ancient Greeks knew long before the invention of the automobile: the right word, especially when it's a verb, can create a specific picture.

Showing rather than just telling in writing is nothing new. The Greeks, for example, believed that writing should be vivid. The term they used was *enargeia*, meaning "visibility." Instead of merely telling the reader, it is the writer's responsibility to show the reader in a way that is as alive, lucid, and palpable as possible. The most effective way to make writing vivid—to show a reader moving pictures—is by focusing on action verbs, words that indicate motion or movement.

Verbs are the engines of every sentence. They create movement and action as well as images that readers can see and hear. Because verbs are so important, students should learn to select verbs with care. They should be able to differentiate between imprecise, passive verbs that suck the life out of sentences and precise, active verbs that enliven them.

The exercises and activities in this chapter help students see and harness the power of verbs to create vigorous, interesting writing. By identifying and learning to distinguish between vapid verbs and vivid ones, students acquire the ability to examine and revise their own sentences with verbs that create writing with more power, more pictures, and more pop. Refer to "Teaching Notes and Answers" for instructional tips and answers.

Chapter 3 Exercises

19. **The Sights and Sounds of Verbs.** This exercise helps students distinguish between two types of vivid action verbs: video verbs (those that add distinctive pictures to writing) and volume verbs (those that create sound effects).

20. **Add Pictures and Sounds.** Students apply their knowledge of vivid verbs by revising sentences to make them more interesting and specific.

21. **Passive Resistance.** This exercise will teach students the difference between active and passive voice and how the use of active voice promotes sentences that are more concise, clear, and compelling.

22. **Zeugma: Last But Not Least.** This exercise introduces a subtle but powerful way to use even weak verbs to add flash to a sentence.

23. **Vivid Verbs, Not Verbosity.** Students revise, focusing on strong, vivid verb selection.

24. **Virtue with Verbs.** Students practice making an abstract idea concrete by using vivid verbs.

25. **I Need Some Advice.** This fun activity helps students harness the power of the verb to write concise, imperative sentences.

19. THE SIGHTS AND SOUNDS OF VERBS

Verbs are the engines of every sentence. They create movement and action as well as images that your reader can see and hear. Because verbs are so important, you should learn to select your verbs with care and to differentiate between imprecise, passive verbs that suck the life out of your sentences, and precise, active verbs that enliven your sentences.

Vivid action verbs come in two major varieties: verbs that provide pictures (video verbs) and verbs that provide a soundtrack (volume verbs).

Video Verbs

clog, scramble, crush, swoon, hurl, weave, dodge, scale, limp, applaud, drag, embrace, snatch, plead, survey, scribble

Volume Verbs

shuffle, bark, sweep, crash, gulp, shout, click, whisper, slam, pound, plop, tap, thud, scratch, drip, dribble, whistle, slurp, flap, splash, thunder

Video verbs paint pictures for the reader: *stroll* rather than *walk*, or *glare* rather than *look*. Volume verbs create sound effects: *slam* instead of *close*, or *slap* instead of *hit*. Carefully inspect each verb you select. Audition each one. Favor the action verb over the state-of-being verb (*is, am, was, were, being*). You don't need to necessarily eliminate every state-of-being verb, but the ratio between state-of-being verbs and action verbs should always favor the vigorous and vivid action verbs.

A volume verb, like any action verb, suggests movement, but it also provides a soundtrack. These verbs take advantage of the rhetorical device called *onomatopoeia*, where the pronunciation of a word imitates a sound, such as *flags flapping*, *birds chirping*, or *doors slamming*. Used judiciously, volume verbs invigorate sentences by stimulating the reader's senses of sound and sight.

Directions

Read the following passage carefully, identifying and circling specific video and vivid verbs used by the writer to bring the past to life.

> *In an earlier, more innocent era, the early 1970s, a time before product warning labels (CAUTION: THIS YO-YO IS NOT TO BE SAUTÉED, STIR-FRIED, OR SWALLOWED!), a unique toy burst onto the market called the Klacker. The toy consisted of two large plastic acrylic balls attached by a length of string. In the middle of the string was a metal ring by which the player could swing and "clack" the balls together. The toy became a sensation. Klacker-playing wannabes congregated at Klacker outlets across the nation, and Klackers flew off store shelves into the eager hands of American children. A cacophony of clacking kids rang out across the land. Klacker craziness was short lived, however. In 1971 the toy was yanked from store shelves because of rampant reports of Klacker injuries. The balls would shatter as they collided, sending shards of Klacker shrapnel into the innocent eyes of children. A Food and Drug Administration ban in the summer of 1971 officially killed the Klacker.*
>
> *Moral: It's only funny until someone has his eye impaled with Klacker shrapnel.*

20. ADD PICTURES AND SOUND

More than any other part of speech, it is the verb that determines whether the writer is a wimp or a wizard. —Constance Hale

Directions

Paying attention to your verbs is a great way to make your sentences more vivid and more interesting. Circle every verb in your drafts, and then ask yourself, "Can I replace this verb with a more vigorous, vivid, vivacious alternative?" Try this out by revising the following sentences, adding more specific video and/or volume verbs.

Example

Original: *The teacher raised his voice, telling the student to sit down.*
Revised: *The teacher's voice thundered as he barked at the student to sit down.*

1. *He quickly drank the glass of cold water.*
2. *The dog looked homeless.*
3. *The dog looked friendly.*
4. *The town was quiet.*
5. *The class worked on its assignment.*
6. *The rain fell heavily.*
7. *Mary looked angry.*
8. *The child was excited.*

21. PASSIVE RESISTANCE

Bill broke the window.

The window was broken by Bill.

Both of these sentences are grammatically correct. But which of the two sentences is better? The answer to this question relates to the issue of the two voices in English: active voice and passive voice. Active voice is the typical, natural voice of English. A subject (Bill) acts directly upon an object (the window).

The second sentence, however, is written in the less common, less natural passive voice, where the subject of the sentence (the window) is acted upon by the object of the sentence (Bill).

As a general rule, the active voice is preferable to the passive voice because the active voice is more direct, more natural, and more concise. Both example sentences say basically the same thing; however, the first sentence, *Bill broke the window*, is stronger because it states what we want to say directly and clearly, using the fewest words.

The active voice helps the writer capitalize on the power of vivid verbs to create action, pictures, and sound. Passive verbs tend to fog meaning and muffle the impact of a sentence. Another liability of the passive voice is the state-of-being verb. The forms of the verb *to be* (*is, was, were, are*) are the most frequently used verbs in English, but they are not active verbs. We certainly need to use them, but if we can eliminate them from a sentence and say the same thing, our writing will become less wordy and more concise.

In addition to helping us make the most of our verbs, the active voice also helps the writer put people in their proper place, as the doers of things. When you have a choice of writing about things versus people, always choose people; after all, remember that you are writing to a person, not a coffee table, a book, or a broken window.

Directions

Revise the following passive sentences by re-writing them in the active voice. Focus on eliminating state-of-being verbs and making people, not things, the subject of the sentences.

1. *The tests were handed back to the students.*

2. *Mistakes were made.*

3. *The students should be commended for their efforts.*

4. *The purchase of a new copy machine was made by the office manager.*

5. *The bowling alley was crowded last Tuesday.*

22. ZEUGMA: LAST BUT NOT LEAST

Verbs are the workhorses of language, but they also have a playful side. The figure of speech called *zeugma* makes a single verb do double-duty by employing the verb in two different senses. Zeugma is the figure of speech that makes your verbs stand out and your readers stand up and take notice.

In the following examples of zeugma, notice how each of the highlighted verbs are used in two completely different ways:

> My mom gave me a list of chores and a splitting headache.

> That little girl always got on the bus and on my nerves.

> Our Thanksgiving dinner filled us with joy, laughter, and a ton of turkey.

Notice that even fairly unexciting verbs like *gave*, *got*, and *filled* become more interesting with zeugma. Notice how the following original sentence becomes much more interesting when the writer revises with zeugma.

> **Original:** *As his relationship with the girl continued, he fell madly in love, but he also began going into debt.*

> **Revised:** *As his relationship with the girl continued, he fell madly in love and deeper in debt.*

Directions

Complete the following sentences using zeugma. First identify the verb, and then finish the sentence by using the verb in a different way than it was used in the first part of the sentence.

1. *My mother lost her car keys and …*

2. *The frustrated teacher gave him a sharpened pencil and …*

3. *If you want to learn to hang-glide, you must be willing to take a course and …*

4. *Jill found the missing assignment and …*

5. *When Bill left his house this morning, he had his lunch box and …*

23. VIVID VERBS, NOT VERBOSITY

Read the following passage, focusing especially on the writer's use of verbs.

> *There's a miraculous invention crafted of metal, wire, and wood that anyone can manipulate to produce his or her own music. My advice to anyone is to chuck your iPod and sprint to your local music store as soon as possible and grab a guitar. No need to buy batteries, update software, or purchase fuel— the acoustic guitar is an old music box that's always new. It sits patiently and quietly in the corner, taking up little room but constantly inviting you to pick it up and strum the stress away. There are a few strings attached—six to be exact—but unlike other musical instruments, you won't need hours of lessons to produce your first recognizable tune; with the guitar, three simple chords are all you'll need to play hundreds of timeless tunes. You can take it anywhere, and unlike with the flute, the trumpet, or the trombone, you can sing while you strum. Every time you play, you'll improve, and because of the limitless possibilities of this six-stringed sonorous sensation, you'll never grow bored. Your fingertips will grow calloused but your heart will soften as you enjoy the soothing sounds you make with this musical miracle.*

Directions

Draw upon your personal experience or insights to answer one of the following questions. Use specific details, insights, anecdotes, and especially vivid verbs to illustrate your central point.

What single moment in your life so far stands out as most memorable? What makes it so unforgettable?

What failure or success has taught you something?

What are you passionate about? Why?

What single piece of advice would you give a person who is two years younger than you?

I. After selecting one of the questions, write a rough draft of at least 200 words.

II. Revise your draft by circling every verb in your draft. Try to replace weak verbs with more vivid alternatives. Also, watch for any instances of passive voice and revise these sentences by recasting the sentences in active voice.

III. Write a final draft that goes beyond just telling your reader. Use active, vivid verbs to show your point.

24. VIRTUE WITH VERBS

Read the following passage about the virtues of being positive. Focus especially on the writer's use of verbs.

A glass that's half-full, a silver lining, the sunny side of life. These may all be clichés, but they're also commonplace reminders that instead of dwelling on the dreary, we should point out the positives. Every child should be taught the virtue of optimism because life is too short to dwell on the negative aspects of life. Imagining possibilities rather than potential pitfalls will help any child tackle the multitude of life's tasks with confidence. And when the child fails, as every child eventually does, she will view defeat as a springboard rather than a one-ton anvil chained to her ankle. Seeing the glass as half-full is not just the idealized fantasy of daydreamers. When Ernest Shackleton's ship, The Endurance, became trapped in the ice on his journey to Antarctica, his dream of traveling across the frozen continent was lost. He might have let failure and hopelessness overwhelm him. The ice eventually crushed his ship, but not his spirit. Shackleton refused to give up. Using every physical, mental, and psychological resource he had, Shackleton and his twenty-seven-man crew struggled tenaciously to survive for twenty-six months. When they finally reached civilization, they had not lost a single man. Buoyed by Shackleton's positive spirit, the expedition snatched victory from the jaws of defeat. Shackleton showed the world that glass-half-full thinking is not just some romantic notion; it's a survival skill.

Directions

What would you argue is an important virtue that parents should teach their children? Why? Explain and illustrate using specific details and vivid verbs to bring your abstract virtue to life. Select from one of the following examples or come up with one of your own.

creativity	*curiosity*	*modesty*
compassion	*manners*	*self-confidence*
humility	*diligence*	*self-discipline*
self-reliance	*faith*	*wisdom*

25. I NEED SOME ADVICE!

Directions

What specific advice would you give to a younger student about how to be successful at your school? Create a list of at least ten pieces of advice. Good advice and strong verbs go hand in hand. State each piece of advice in the form of a command, a complete imperative sentence. Focus especially on using specific, vivid verbs.

Use this list to spark your own ideas.

1. *Set goals, stay organized, and fight procrastination.*
2. *Choose silence over obnoxiousness.*
3. *Think before you speak; listen before you answer.*
4. *Jump right back up when you fall down.*
5. *Support and cheer an unsung sports team.*
6. *Don't plan your future around your boyfriend or girlfriend.*
7. *Befriend foreign exchange students.*
8. *Don't take good friends, good teachers, or good parents for granted.*
9. *Take charge of your attitude; don't let others choose it for you.*
10. *Sit by someone new at lunch today; don't live the same life every day.*

19. THE SIGHTS AND SOUNDS OF VERBS

Verbs can evoke any of the five senses, but most English verbs appeal to the senses of sight and sound.

Consider opening this activity by showing students the following quote and asking them if they agree with Donald Hall's assertion that verbs are the most important part of speech in English. There certainly is no single right answer to this question, but the key is to help students understand that paying attention to the verbs they use in writing will make a difference. After all, just try to write a complete sentence without one.

> *Verbs act. Verbs move. Verbs do. Verbs strike, soothe, grin, cry, exasperate, decline, fly, hurt, and heal. Verbs make writing go, and they matter more to our language than any other part of speech.* —Donald Hall

After completing the activity, you might read the following passage aloud, asking students to listen carefully for the volume verbs they hear.

> *Doubt has many voices. It <u>whispers</u> in your ear, rudely interrupting your confident thoughts just before a big test. You can hear doubt <u>murmuring</u> in the corner when you step to the podium to give your prepared speech. The voice of doubt <u>mutters</u> quietly at first, but gradually grows to a <u>roar</u> as you approach Mary at her locker to ask her to the dance. Sometimes, however, you're able to tune out the voice of doubt. It's <u>screaming</u> in your ear, but you ignore it, and sink the winning basket to win the city championship.*

The action verbs are underlined in the following passage. Most are video verbs, but the verbs *burst, clack, rang,* and *shatter* are volume verbs.

> *From an earlier, more innocent era, the early 1970s, a time before product warning labels (CAUTION: THIS YO-YO IS NOT TO BE <u>SAUTÉED</u>, <u>STIR-FRIED</u>, OR <u>SWALLOWED</u>!), a unique toy <u>burst</u> onto the market called the Klacker. The toy <u>consisted</u> of two large plastic acrylic balls <u>attached</u> by a length of string. In the middle of the string was a metal ring by which the player could <u>swing</u> and "<u>clack</u>" the balls together. The toy became a sensation. Klacker-playing wannabes <u>congregated</u> at Klacker outlets across the nation, and Klackers <u>flew</u> off store shelves into the eager hands of American children. A cacophony of clacking kids <u>rang</u> out across the land. Klacker craziness was short-lived, however. In 1971 the toy was <u>yanked</u> from store shelves because of rampant reports of Klacker injuries. The balls would <u>shatter</u> as they <u>collided</u>, sending shards of Klacker shrapnel into the innocent eyes of children. A Food and Drug Administration ban in the summer of 1971 officially <u>killed</u> the Klacker.*

> *Moral: It's only funny until someone has his eye <u>impaled</u> with Klacker shrapnel.*

20. ADD PICTURES AND SOUND

Before students complete this activity, point out the original and revised sentences in the example. Although the two sentences are similar, students should notice that the difference in the choice of verbs makes the revised sentence much more effective.

Possible Answers

1. *He guzzled the cold glass of water, pausing only to momentarily gulp and wipe the dripping water from his chin.*
2. *The mangy mutt limped down the street, whimpering with each step.*
3. *With its wildly wagging tail and perpetually panting tongue, the dog was hard to resist.*
4. *A gentle breeze blowing the fallen leaves of autumn along the streets was the only audible sound as the sun set on the small town.*
5. *The twenty-five sophomores sat hovered over their desks; the only sound heard in the classroom was frenetic scribbling of No. 2 pencils on paper.*
6. *The rattle of the relentless rain against the windows was so loud that it caused the family dog, Huck, to race to the front door expecting an intruder.*
7. *Mary slammed her fist on the desk, lowered her eyebrows into an indignant glare, and stomped out of the room.*
8. *Sally quivered with delight and screeched with joy when her father announced that the family was going to Disneyland.*

21. PASSIVE RESISTANCE

Before handing out the worksheet, you might put the following two sentences on the board. Then ask students which of the two sentences is better and why:

> *The book was read by Mary.*

> *Mary read the book.*

Students may not know the terms active and passive voice, but they probably will have an intuitive sense that the more direct and concise sentence (the second one) is the better sentence. Point out that writing in the active voice allows us to eliminate the helping verb *was*, leaving the single active verb, *read*, to directly state that Mary is the doer of the action.

After briefly introducing this concept, give students the worksheet and have them read through the explanations provided, which specifically articulate the differences between active and passive voice. Then have students revise the passive sentences, putting them into the active voice. You should also point out that as a general rule, we should prefer the active to the passive; however, there are times when the passive voice is necessary. For example, sometimes you want to focus on things over people. If you just ate a delicious apple, for example, it would be natural to say, *The apple was delicious* instead of saying the wordier alternative, *I just ate a delicious apple*.

Possible Answers

1. *The teacher handed the tests back to the students.*
2. *We made mistakes.*
3. *The principal should commend her students for their efforts.*
4. *The office manager purchased a new copy machine.*
5. *People crowded the bowling alley last Tuesday.*

22. ZEUGMA: LAST BUT NOT LEAST

Before handing out this worksheet, write the following two sentences on the board and ask students to identify anything unusual about them.

My mom gave me a list of chores and a splitting headache.

That little girl always got on the bus and on my nerves.

Students have probably never heard of zeugma, but they might notice the way in which the verbs "gave" and "got" are used in two different senses. If they don't notice this at first, circle the verbs, and ask if they notice anything about how the verbs are used in the sentences. Next, pass out the worksheet and guide students through the opening explanation and examples before they complete the sample sentences provided.

Possible Answers

1. *My mother lost her car keys and her temper.*
2. *The frustrated teacher gave him a sharpened pencil and a lecture on being prepared for class.*
3. *If you want to learn to hang-glide, you must be willing to take a course and your life in your hands.*
4. *Jill found the missing assignment and a new upbeat attitude.*
5. *When Bill left his house this morning, he had his lunch box and a bad headache.*

23. VIVID VERBS, NOT VERBOSITY

Begin by giving students the worksheet and reading the model paragraph. As you read, students circle specific verbs that help the passage come alive for the reader. Ask students to share what they notice.

Next, have students select one of the topics and follow the writing process outlined in the directions to write and revise their own paragraphs. Students can peer review their work with partners or in small groups, using Step 2 of the activity to focus on alternative choices for specific verbs.

24. VIRTUE WITH VERBS

After students read the paragraph, discuss how the writer uses verbs to bring the abstract idea of "optimism" to life using vivid verbs as well as other details. Students should notice that the idea of "optimism" is brought to life by the writer's description of the specific actions of specific people. Thus, the reader can see what is meant by the abstract ideas through the writer's use of concrete details.

This discussion equips students to write their own paragraphs, using vivid verbs to bring an abstract virtue to life. Plan time to allow students to share their paragraphs in small groups or in whole-class presentations.

25. I NEED SOME ADVICE!

Use the list of advice on the worksheet as a model for this activity. Before students write their own advice, have them read the examples provided on the worksheet. Ask students to share what they notice about the role vivid verbs play in the list. If students don't notice, point out that several of the sentences contain multiple verbs; this gives the ten sentences more variety. Challenge students to construct varied sentences as they begin to write their own lists of ten pieces of advice.

Concrete Nouns—Knee-high Tube Socks, a Brown Bag, and a Splash of Salt Water

KEY TERMS

Abstract Noun: An idea that can't be perceived by the senses, such as *bravery*, *dedication*, *excellence*, or *anxiety*.

Concrete Noun: A person, place, or thing that can be held or touched by your hand, such as *knee-high tube socks*, *a brown bag*, or *a splash of salt water*.

THE WHAT, WHY, AND HOW OF CONCRETE NOUNS

What is the single key difference between average writers and skilled ones? Is there some mysterious secret that sets their writing apart?

The truth is that every accomplished writer understands the importance of concrete nouns. Look at the following passage, for example. There is nothing mysterious about concrete nouns. They are as plain as the nose on your face, or the pencil in your hand, or the shoe on your foot. And as effective as a hammer hitting a nail true.

> *A nimble thumb controlled by a numb mind hovers over a television remote. The television picture flickers as channels flash by: CNN, ESPN, the Game Show Network, the Home Shopping Network. A young mind, once sound and sharp, slowly turns to mush. Muscles atrophy and the waistline expands as another victim is entranced by the TV's mesmerizing glow. America's young need more reading, more exercise, and less television. Brains need to be fed by physical and intellectual activity, instead of being starved by Technicolor trash.*

Good writing balances the general and the specific, the abstract and the concrete. Too often, however, the writing scale weighs on the heavy abstract and general side. The cure for this is concrete nouns. A concrete noun is a person, place, or thing that can be held or touched by your hand: knee-high tube socks, a brown bag, or a splash of salt water.

Concrete nouns help students move from just telling the reader to showing the reader specific, detailed pictures. Readers want details that can be seen, smelled, touched, tasted, and heard. Professional writers move up and down the Ladder of Abstraction (see the following explanation) and they know that keeping a reader interested requires spending a significant amount of time on the bottom rung, talking about real people, real places, and real things.

Exercises in this chapter will give students practice in applying this valuable writing skill. Refer to "Teaching Notes and Answers" at the end of the chapter for specific instructional tips and answers.

Chapter 4 Exercises

26. **Pouring Concrete.** This exercise introduces students to the concrete noun and gives them practice transforming telling sentences into showing sentences.

27. **The Ladder of Abstraction.** Students learn about the Ladder of Abstraction, a way of visualizing the movement of language from abstract, general words to concrete, specific words.

28. **Abstract to Concrete.** Students practice how to make an abstract idea come to life by using concrete nouns.

29. **Concrete Hook and Full-circle Conclusion.** This exercise introduces an effective strategy for effective introductions and conclusions.

30. **Wish You Were Here.** This writing activity challenges students to describe a specific place using concrete details.

31. **The Big Hassle.** This writing activity calls on students to respond to a specific question by including details on the bottom rung of the Ladder of Abstraction.

32. **Horoscope Hilarity.** With this fun activity, students experience firsthand the difference between vague, general writing and writing that is packed with specific details.

26. POURING CONCRETE

A concrete noun is a person, place, or thing that can be held or touched by your hand: knee-high tube socks, a brown bag, or a splash of salt water. Readers hunger for details that can be seen, smelled, touched, tasted, or heard. Concrete nouns keep the reader alert and interested by painting sensory pictures. If you're talking about justice, describe the wooden gavel and the slapping sound it makes as the judge punctuates his verdict. If you're talking about eating lunch, identify what kind of sandwich you ate. If you're talking about the benefits of technology, mention the brand of your computer, the size of your computer screen, or the name of your favorite website. Concrete nouns provide particular pictures to go along with abstract ideas. They're the seasoning you add to make your sentences more than just bland, boring buffet food.

To see the differences, compare the following sentences. The original example is pretty straightforward and devoid of many concrete nouns. The revised version, in contrast, comes alive because of the plentiful concrete nouns that provide a more detailed picture for the reader.

Original: *My grandfather recited poetry as he did his chores.*

Revised: *As a boy in the 1940s, I stood in the tie-up watching my New Hampshire grandfather milk Holsteins while reciting poems for my entertainment. His hands stripped milk to the poem's beat. He threw back his head, rolled his eyes in high drama and pounded out: "But there is no joy in Mudville—mighty Casey has struck out." —Donald Hall, "Bring Back the Out-Loud Culture." Newsweek, 15 April 1985.*

Concrete nouns make your writing stand out from the crowd. With specific, concrete nouns you add details your reader can see. The portrait you paint with words is distinct and alive.

Directions

Revise the following sentences by adding at least three specific, concrete nouns that provide the reader with a more detailed and specific picture.

Example

Original: *He ate dinner alone.*

Revised: *He sat alone, eating his dinner, a T-bone steak with white rice and a glass of flat root beer.*

1. *The room was a mess.*

2. *She sat quietly reading.*

3. *The rain fell.*

4. *The children played.*

5. *The sun came up.*

27. THE LADDER OF ABSTRACTION

Liberty is an abstract idea. You can hold the idea in your mind but not in your hand. Notice how Lincoln, in the following quotation, uses concrete nouns to ground his idea about liberty with details that the reader can see, hear, smell, taste, or touch.

> *The shepherd drives the wolf from the sheep's throat, for which the sheep thanks the shepherd as his liberator, while the wolf denounces him for the same act as the destroyer of liberty. —Abraham Lincoln*

The Ladder of Abstraction is one way to visualize the range of language from the abstract to the concrete—from the general to the specific. On the top of the ladder are abstract ideas like success, education, or freedom; as we move down each rung of the ladder the words become more specific and more concrete. When we reach the bottom rung of the Ladder of Abstraction, we should find something that we can see or touch, hear, taste, or smell.

Example

5TH RUNG	EDUCATION	NOURISHMENT	THE ECONOMY
4TH RUNG	Core subjects	Food	Finances
3RD RUNG	Mathematics	Italian food	Money
2ND RUNG	Algebra	Lasagna	Coins
1ST RUNG	Algebra 2 class	Mr. Johnson's roasted vegetable lasagna	A 1972 Lincoln penny

In the example above, at the bottom rung of the Ladder of Abstraction, you'll find the most specific, concrete idea, an idea that invokes one or more of your reader's five senses. When you are writing, remember the bottom rung of the Ladder of Abstraction; it rests on a strong, concrete foundation.

Directions

Practice moving up and down the Ladder of Abstraction by completing the following table.

5TH RUNG	RECREATION	CIVILIZATION	FREEDOM
4TH RUNG			
3RD RUNG			
2ND RUNG			
1ST RUNG			

28. ABSTRACT TO CONCRETE

Good writers do as much showing as they do telling. The secret to showing is using concrete nouns to create pictures for your reader. Circle every concrete noun in your draft. The test is this: is it a person, place, or thing that can be touched or felt by your hand? In most cases, proper nouns are concrete, such as Kleenex, Abraham Lincoln, and Mount Rushmore, but so are many lowercase nouns, such as dog, rain, table, shoulder, and tongue depressor. Add specific details and specific pictures for your reader by revising sentences to make abstract or general words concrete.

For example, notice how the following two passages reveal the abstract ideas of fear and failure, respectively, by describing a specific scene made up of concrete people, places, and things.

> After throwing the enormous, dripping spit-wad, Luke cowered under his desk as the pounding footsteps of the angry teacher reverberated through the classroom. Balling himself up into a fetal position, Luke closed his eyes and put his hands over his ears.

> As Mrs. Smith passed back the math tests, she avoided eye contact with Mary. At that point Mary knew without even looking at her paper that she had the lowest grade in the class. She sank into her seat and began to pray for the bell to ring.

Directions

Select one of the following abstract nouns listed. Then ask yourself, "What does this idea look like in the real, concrete world?" Write one or more sentences where you make the abstract noun come to life by describing a specific scene using concrete nouns at the bottom rung of the Ladder of Abstraction. Don't use the abstract noun in your sentence; instead, show the idea behind the word through specific, concrete description and word choice.

intelligence	stupidity	success	joy	truth
victory	defeat	the past	the future	bravery
diligence	procrastination	war	peace	imagination
power	poverty	education	loyalty	tradition

Abstract Idea: _____

Specific Scene:

_____

_____

_____

29. CONCRETE HOOK AND FULL-CIRCLE CONCLUSION

The introduction and conclusion of any essay are vital. The introduction hooks the reader, capturing attention; a good ending wraps the essay up for the reader in a satisfying way.

Concrete Hook. Make a strong first impression on your reader by beginning on the bottom rung of the Ladder of Abstraction, talking about concrete, specific people, places, and things. Starting with concrete nouns will hook the reader's interest by providing concrete images of real people, places, and things. Using a concrete hook is a great way to introduce the relevance of your idea in the real world by showing rather than telling. A concrete hook also opens the door for ending your composition with a smooth, satisfying conclusion.

Full-circle Conclusion. When you wrap up your essay, return to your opening concrete image or scene to give your reader the pleasing sense of coming full circle. Returning to the starting point will give the reader the satisfying, almost subliminal, feeling of completing a journey successfully.

Directions

Read the following passage about the idea of learning. As you read, notice how the writer employs both a concrete hook and a full-circle conclusion:

> A grade is a carrot that dangles from a piece of string in front of our faces, reminding us to keep moving toward our goal. Unfortunately, that goal is too often just completing the class so that we can move on to another class, or completing an assignment so that we can move on to the next one. Learning should be a smorgasbord where we can feast on our passion for learning, not just working to finish a class, but instead immersing ourselves in the learning process to emerge as a different and better person because of what we have learned. Learning rather than grades should be our focus because true learning whets our appetite for more and creates a passion that is insatiable. Grades, in contrast, are artificial, external rewards that shift our focus from true knowledge to a few simple letters of the alphabet. For example, a student who reads Hamlet for a grade will read superficially and learn only a few memorable quotes, such as "Brevity is the soul of wit." A student who truly learns Hamlet, however, will see the irony in this quote: "Polonius the long-winded sycophant of the illegitimate king has neither wit nor brevity." He exemplifies the kind of people that Hamlet despises: people who waste words indiscriminately, people who speak to impress rather than to the point, and people who love to hear themselves talk rather than listen to others. A student who is truly learning will take time to understand the genius of Shakespeare's great characters, great words, and great drama. This student will drink deep from the fountain of knowledge and will still thirst to learn more. Instead of finding a carrot dangling in front of his nose, he or she will find multi-faceted carats of knowledge that will remain valuable forever.

1. What concrete nouns does the writer use in the first sentence?
2. What concrete noun does the writer refer to in the concluding sentence to bring the reader full circle?
3. As a reader, how would you describe the effect of the writer's use of a concrete hook and a full-circle conclusion?
4. Now select your own topic from the list your teacher gives you. Write an introductory paragraph where you address the question using a concrete hook.

30. WISH YOU WERE HERE

Directions

Write a description of a place or event that you think a specific group should visit. Some ideas for groups you could use include teenagers, teachers, heavy metal fans, or sports fans.

Make sure that both the group and the place or event are ones that you know something about; then use detailed description and concrete nouns to both tell and show what is so special about this place or event. Also, use a concrete hook and a full-circle conclusion.

Example

The pageantry, the mystery, the Flying Saucer Pancake Eating Contest. This is one annual event that every believer in UFOs must attend: the Roswell UFO Encounter held each year during the first week of July in Roswell, New Mexico. Any UFO buff already knows the story: on the night of July 8, 1947, something crashed twenty miles north of Roswell. Was it a flying saucer? Was it a weather balloon? We may never know. But ever since that faithful night, Roswell has been ground zero for people who are fascinated by alien abduction, alien autopsies, and alien belt buckles. Visitors to this annual paradise of the paranormal enjoy a UFO lecture series, participate in the Alien Costume Contest, and gather to watch the Galactic Grand Prix parade of homemade spaceships. Maybe they've been out in the sun too long; after all, it is pretty hot in New Mexico in July. Then again, maybe they are just curious to solve the mystery of whether we are truly alone in this universe.

_____

_____

_____

_____

_____

_____

_____

_____

_____

_____

31. THE BIG HASSLE

I don't have pet peeves; I have whole kennels of irritations. —Whoopi Goldberg

What would you argue is one of the biggest hassles of modern life? Write a paragraph of at least 120 words describing your biggest hassle. Use at least ten concrete nouns that show your reader why it truly is a big hassle. Also, use a concrete hook and a full-circle conclusion.

Example

Abraham Lincoln died in 1865, but I see him everywhere I go. Something must be done immediately! Everywhere I look, everywhere I walk in my home I seem to run into them, the scattered scourge of orphan Lincoln pennies. They clutter the kitchen counter, they clog the vacuum, they clang around as they fall from every windowsill and tabletop I encounter. Something must be done now to stop this pandemic of pennies. Can you even buy anything with a penny anymore? Can't we just round up to the more sensible five-cent piece, the nickel? Not that I have anything against Honest Abe; I'm sure he was a great guy—speaking eloquently at Gettysburg, saving the Union, wearing distinctive hats—but he's become so ubiquitous that it's ridiculous! The Lincoln penny has become a royal pain.

32. HOROSCOPE HILARITY

Horoscopes are an example of writing that is full of generalities. The horoscope writer provides readers with a broad outline—so broad that just about any reader can apply these vague statements to the specific events of his or her life. Your mission is to take one of these general horoscopes and enhance it with specific, concrete details that reveal what would happen if the events played out in the real world. Focus on being as specific as possible, and use plenty of concrete nouns.

Example

Original: Today may mark a red-letter day for you concerning your work or career. An important development may transpire that will have a direct effect on bettering your earnings.

Concrete follow-up: In fact, today as you're working at your dishwashing job at The Big Lobster, your boss, Bob Hurlbutt, will approach you as you're scraping food off a ten-foot stack of plates. He'll say, "Hey Joe. Larry just quit. I need you to take over his job as the doorman. It's not very hard work. You just open the door when someone approaches. They usually hand you a tip as they pass by, so wear pants with deep pockets. Oh, yeah, I almost forgot to mention, it pays twice what you are currently earning per hour."

Directions

Select one of the following horoscopes. Read it carefully, looking for generalities that can be transformed into specific details. Write a concrete follow-up of at least eighty words, with at least eight concrete nouns. If you are working with a class, compare your "concrete follow-up" with someone who used the same original horoscope.

If there is something you would like to be more involved in, today may be the day to make your move. Don't wait to be asked, go after it. In fact ...

Your ideas and thinking are likely to have a greater influence over your peers today than you might realize. Don't discount what you have to offer before you get a chance to express things. In fact ...

You stand a very good chance today of satisfactorily wrapping up a matter that has caused you some contention recently. If need be, press the situation. In fact ...

Just because at first glance something appears to be tedious or tough doesn't necessarily mean it will turn out to be so. In fact, you'll operate at your best today when faced with a challenge ...

Thank goodness you've got your head screwed on tight because early disruptions could put you in a dither today. You, however, will tame the lion and bring about the results you desire. In fact ...

Chapter 4 Teaching Notes and Answers

26. POURING CONCRETE

To introduce this activity, put the following two sentences on the board.

> *Version One*
> *A group of people was gathered at the door to the prison.*
>
> *Version Two*
> *A throng of bearded men, in sad-colored garments and gray, steeple-crowned hats, intermixed with women, some wearing hoods, and others bareheaded, was assembled in front of a wooden edifice, the door of which was heavily timbered with oak, and studded with iron spikes. —Nathaniel Hawthorne, The Scarlet Letter*

Ask students, "What are some examples of specific details in Version Two that show the reader a more detailed picture?" Point out, by way of introduction, that one of the key differences that separate good writing from average writing is the writer's use of concrete nouns. As students revise the sentences in this activity, take some time to have individual students share. It is exciting for students to see how one simple sentence can be revised in so many different ways.

Sample Revisions

1. *Strewn clothes, an unmade bed, and scattered trash caused Bill's mom to officially declare his room a disaster area.*

2. *Mary sat motionless in the overstuffed chair, transfixed by the latest adventures of Harry Potter.*

3. *The rain fell. From 2:00 a.m. until 4:00 a.m., the rain fell in buckets, pelting the roof so hard that it woke the entire house.*

4. *The giggling first graders played four-square in the brand new playground. Children played across the street from the Senior Center.*

5. *The sun rose like a sleeping giant, emerging from the snowy peaks of Mount Baker.*

27. THE LADDER OF ABSTRACTION

Introduce this activity by showing students one or both of the following quotations.

> *The tree of liberty must be refreshed from time to time with the blood of patriots and tyrants. It is its natural manure. —Thomas Jefferson*
>
> *Those who profess to favor freedom, and yet depreciate agitation are men who want rain without thunder and lighting. —Frederick Douglas*

Ask students: "How do these writers go beyond just telling us about 'liberty' and 'freedom,' to showing us a specific picture?" Students should notice that the writers' use of concrete nouns provides the reader with details that the reader can see (blood), hear (thunder), and possibly even smell (manure).

After handing out the worksheet, guide students through its explanation of the Ladder of Abstraction. Before students complete the table provided, you might take some time to complete one of the ladders together as a class.

Possible Answers

5TH RUNG	RECREATION	CIVILIZATION	FREEDOM
4TH RUNG	Sports	Government	Free speech
3RD RUNG	Baseball	State capital	First Amendment
2ND RUNG	Seattle Mariners	Olympia, Washington	Protestors
1ST RUNG	Ichiro Suzuki	Capitol dome of Olympia, Washington	Signs saying "Boycott Wal-Mart"

28. ABSTRACT TO CONCRETE

See the example passages on fear and failure as models for this activity. Before passing out this worksheet, read one of the example passages aloud to the class.

Ask: "What abstract idea would you say the writer is describing in this passage?" Read the passage a couple of times, and call on students to share their ideas. As you pass out the worksheet, explain that writers make abstract ideas come alive for their readers by using concrete nouns. As students write their own passages, have them share with each other and the class, to test whether or not their use of concrete language conveys the full sense of the abstract idea.

29. CONCRETE HOOK AND FULL-CIRCLE CONCLUSION

To introduce this activity, show students the following passage: the first and last sentences of Lincoln's "Gettysburg Address." Ask them: "What words or themes does Lincoln use to link his introductory sentence to his concluding sentence?"

> *Four score and seven years ago our fathers brought forth on this continent, a new nation, conceived in Liberty, and dedicated to the proposition that all men are created equal.*

> *It is rather for us to be here dedicated to the great task remaining before us— that from these honored dead we take increased devotion to that cause for which they gave the last full measure of devotion—that we here highly resolve that these dead shall not have died in vain—that this nation, under God, shall have a new birth of freedom—and that government of the people, by the people, for the people, shall not perish from the earth.*

If students read closely, they will notice the repetition of the words "dedicated," "nation," and "new" in both sentences. They might also notice the similar themes of "freedom" and "liberty," and "conceived" and "new birth." Explain to students that great writers and great speechwriters, like Lincoln, know the importance of beginnings and endings, and they know the power of linking an introduction and a conclusion to bring the reader full circle.

Follow this activity by giving students the worksheet. Have them read through the paragraph, answering the three questions that follow before they write their own paragraph.

Answers

1. carrot, piece of string, face
2. carrot

30. WISH YOU WERE HERE

Give students the handout, and read the example as a model. Ask students: "How does the writer's use of concrete nouns help to show you, the reader, what this event is like?" Spend some time in class pointing out specific details in the model before students begin writing their own compositions. Students can revise their pieces with peers or in small groups. Also, plan time for them to share their final products.

31. THE BIG HASSLE

Before giving students this handout, write the question on the board: "What would you argue is one of the biggest hassles of modern life?" Invite students to brainstorm a list that includes multiple answers. Once you have a list of 15–20 items based on student ideas, give students the handout and read the example. Ask students to point out specific nouns that support their answers. Students should then use their brainstormed lists for ideas to write their own paragraphs.

32. HOROSCOPE HILARITY

To introduce this activity, you might read a daily horoscope from a local paper. Ask students if they would consider horoscopes good writing. If not, what would improve them? Then pass out the handout and have students compare the original horoscope with the concrete follow-up. Next, have them select one of the five horoscopes listed and write their own concrete follow-ups using plenty of concrete nouns. Since students will want to share these, plan time for student to read their pieces in small groups or to the entire class.

CHAPTER 5

Lists—The Parade of Particulars

KEY TERMS

Asyndeton: The omission of conjunctions in a series of words, phrases, or clauses, such as: *I came, I saw, I conquered.*

Hyphenated modifier: The use of hyphenated words, besides just adjectives, to modify a noun, such as: *He's one of those I-never-arrive-less-than-five-minutes-late-to-class students.*

Polysyndeton: An addition of conjunctions in a series of words, phrases, or clauses, such as: *I came and I saw and I conquered.*

THE WHAT, HOW, AND WHY OF LISTS

Bacon-asparagus quiche, bacon-wrapped turkey, hot bacon salad dressing, barbeque baked beans with bacon, dark chocolate infused with the flavor of applewood-smoked bacon, corn and bacon chowder, maple-bacon pancakes, bacon-wrapped, deep-fried hot dogs, potato chips with bacon dip, bacon bits, caramelized bacon, bacon biscuits, lamb's brains with bacon and apple butter ... Do you see where I'm going here?

Bacon. It's what's for breakfast, lunch, and dinner.

Anyone reading this list gets the point: Bacon comes in an astonishingly large number of pleasing and curious varieties. If you're a carnivore, your mouth is probably watering.

"Details, details, details" should be the writer's mantra, and lists are one tool that writers use to shovel up heaping helpings of savory details for the reader to enjoy.

Why is a simple list like the one that opens this chapter so effective for writing? The answer is simple but also profound: It appeals to the reader's need for particular concrete detail. Too often writers dwell too much on abstractions and generalities. Granted, abstractions are important; after all, one of the qualities that make us human is our ability to think abstractly. However, as humans we also have two feet firmly planted on the cold, hard ground. We live in physical surroundings, so we need a balance of the abstract and the concrete as well as the general and the specific. We can be told many things, but we prefer to see, hear, taste, smell, and feel things for ourselves.

The exercises and writing assignments in this chapter expose students to a wide variety of examples. Students will see lists in action as they get valuable experience applying lists in writing. In addition, students will learn the subtle techniques for list-making, such as polysyndeton, asyndeton, and hyphenated modifiers.

Chapter 5 Exercises

33. **Listmania.** This exercise will introduce students to examples of lists and give them an opportunity to begin experimenting with their own.

34. **Asyndeton and Polysyndeton.** Practice manipulating conjunctions for desired effect.

35. **Hyphenated Modifier.** This exercise will introduce students to a magical method of turning just about any word into a noun modifier. This simple but fun technique will add spice, spunk, and a touch of silliness to their sentences.

36. **In Praise of ...** Students apply what they have learned about lists by writing about a topic they are enthusiastic about.

37. **Defining Abstractions.** This writing task challenges students to transform an abstraction into something concrete by defining it in concrete terms.

38. **Chamber of Commerce Description.** This fun activity will allow students to use hype or hyperbole to write about a place they know well.

33. LISTMANIA

Notice how the following paragraph employs a list—a catalog of concrete details—to help the reader understand and empathize with the daily hassles of the average teenager.

> *Being a teenager means dealing with the daily slings and arrows of outrageous fortune: school lunches, your dog eating your homework, too much homework, too little sleep, unrequited love, popping a zit and then forgetting to maintain it so it bleeds all over your face, paper cuts, grades posted on the Internet, bad hair days, being picked last in gym, walking into the wrong bathroom, forgetting your locker combination, not realizing that there are questions on the back of the test, testy I-don't-care-what-excuse-you-have-for-being-late-to-class teachers, calling someone the wrong name but not realizing it until after they have left the room, embarrassing yearbook photos, having everything on the test be everything you didn't study, reading* Hamlet.

So how can a writer meet the reader's need for the concrete? One simple way is to include a list of specific, concrete nouns: things that can be held in your hand or touched. Practice producing parades of particulars and compiling catalogs of the concrete.

You don't necessarily need long lists. Shorter lists can be just as effective. Here are some examples.

Robert J. Samuelson writing in Newsweek about living in an age of technology:

> *No one remembers life before cars, TVs, air conditioners, jets, credit cards, microwave ovens, and ATM cards.*

Later, Samuelson lists a parade of professions that have benefited from the invention of cell phones:

> *For those constantly on the road (salesmen, real-estate agents, repair technicians, some managers and reporters), [cell phones] are a godsend.*

Directions

Generating your own lists of particulars related to a specific topic is a great way to practice using concrete, specific details in your writing. Select three of the following topics and generate lists of at least five items for each topic. Write your lists in complete sentences.

Things in my room.	*Things I need to do by tomorrow.*
Songs on my iPod.	*Important numbers in my life.*
Places I want to visit before I die.	*Brand names of items I have in my home.*
Nicknames I've had in my life.	*Inventory of the things in my locker.*
Presents I've received.	*Jobs I'd hate to have.*
Holidays I'd like to invent.	*Things that we love to hate.*
Strange but delicious foods.	*Famous people who are also infamous.*
Names of the pets I've had in my life.	

34. ASYNDETON AND POLYSYNDETON

Most lists use a final conjunction to signal the last element, such as apples, oranges, and bananas.

Some lists, however, omit the conjunction to give the reader the feeling that list goes on and on indefinitely, such as apples, oranges, bananas, grapes.

This subtle, yet powerful technique is called asyndeton. Notice how George Orwell uses asyndeton to capture the overwhelming abundance of food from the perspective of a man who is poor and hungry:

> *Everywhere there is food insulting you in huge, wasteful piles; whole dead pigs, baskets of hot loaves, great yellow blocks of butter, strings of sausages, mountains of potatoes, vast Gruyere cheeses like grindstones.*

Instead of eliminating conjunctions, some writers exercise another option: inserting a conjunction after each item, such as apples and oranges and bananas and grapes.

This technique is called polysyndeton. The added conjunctions slow the list down and place special emphasis on each one. The repetition of conjunctions gives the reader the feeling that things are piling up, and often places a dramatic emphasis on each item in the list, as in these examples:

> *Just remember this, Mr. Potter: that this rabble you're talking about, they do most of the working and paying and living and dying in this community.*
> *—Jimmy Stewart as George Bailey in It's a Wonderful Life*

Directions

Expand the following sentence stems using both asyndeton and polysyndeton. As you expand the sentences, decide which versions sound the best.

> *Original: I have so many things to do tomorrow: I have to mow the lawn ...*

> *Asyndeton: I have so many things to do tomorrow: I have to mow the lawn, wash the car, paint the back fence, fix the garage door.*

> *Polysyndeton: I have so many things to do tomorrow: I have to mow the lawn and wash the car and paint the back fence and fix the garage door.*

1. *The rumor spread everywhere in a matter of minutes: to the cafeteria ...*
2. *His locker was filled to the brim with textbooks ...*
3. *The picture on the television flickers as channels flash by: CNN ...*
4. *We will travel to Los Angeles ...*
5. *The meal was excellent. We ate ...*

35. HYPHENATED MODIFIER

In typical English sentences we use adjectives to modify nouns. However, there's a little-known, seldom-used, anything-but-everyday device used by writers to transform just about any word into a noun modifier. The device is called the hyphenated modifier. Writers use it to pack more specific detail into their sentences and to add a touch of playfulness and distinctiveness—their own voices—to their essays. You can use the hyphenated modifier to transform a run-of-the-mill, so-boring-it-puts-your-reader-to-sleep sentence into a fresh and fun-to-read sentence. These quirky coagulations of language, used judiciously, can make your reader sit up and maybe even smile.

Notice, for example, how the following sentences are revised using hyphenated modifiers.

> Original: She hasn't read anything but Harry Potter books for the past five years.

> Revised: She's one of those I-haven't-read-anything-but-a-Harry-Potter-book-in-five-years students.

> Original: He's one of those students who is always late to first period.

> Revised: He's one of those I-never-arrive-less-than-five-minutes-late-to-first-period students.

Directions

Add hyphenated modifiers to fill in the holes in the following sentences.

1. *Our substitute teacher gave us a _____ assignment.*

2. *His mother is frustrated with his _____ attitude.*

3. *When I asked for a raise, my boss gave me one of those _____ looks.*

4. *Whenever we go camping, my dad tells us _____ stories.*

5. *Mary always wins at tennis because she has a _____ attitude.*

6. *She always listens to _____ songs on her iPod.*

7. *He wrote a terrible review of the film, calling it "one of those _____ movies."*

8. *The salesman said it was a _____ car, but Jerry bought it anyway.*

36. IN PRAISE OF...

Directions

Select a topic that you feel extremely positive about and write a composition in which you explain why you think it is so wonderful: your favorite food, your favorite website, your favorite day of the week, your favorite teacher. Incorporate lists of particulars into your explanation, using asyndeton, polysyndeton, or hyphenated modifiers as appropriate. Write at least 200 words, and provide at least ten different reasons.

Example

I love the Beatles because even though they were four ordinary working-class lads from Liverpool, England, they managed to change music and culture forever; because even though they were more famous and sold more records than Elvis and Michael Jackson, they never lost the common touch, the common vernacular, or their minds; because even though they were not classically trained musicians, they didn't allow their ignorance to hinder them; instead, they used it as a steppingstone to question and challenge conventions in music; because the band's name is a pun, and their lyrics reflect a love of playing with language: "Yellow-matter custard, dripping from a dead dog's eye!"; because they were not an overnight success: they worked for years in obscurity to hone their craft; because even when they achieved the phenomenal, girls-pulling-their-hair-out-and-screaming-their-lungs-out success of Beatlemania, they still strove to play better, to write better songs, to break new ground; because no two Beatles songs sound the same; because the friendly song-writing competition between John Lennon and Paul McCartney spurred both of them to write better and better songs: "Yesterday," "In My Life," "Eleanor Rigby," "Strawberry Fields Forever"; because even though George Harrison contributed unforgettable guitar riffs to Paul and John's songs, he developed into a great song writer in his own right; because even though Ringo wasn't a song writer, he inspired his mates with a steady beat and his creative malapropisms: "It's been a hard day's night"; because when you listen to a Beatles song today, it sounds as fresh and vibrant as the day it was first recorded; because a four-year old who hears his first Beatles song this morning will still be humming it as he's tucked into bed by his parents tonight.

37. DEFINING ABSTRACTIONS

Notice how the following paragraph illustrates the abstract idea of honesty. After introducing the idea, the paragraph unleashes a parade of particulars that gives the reader multiple pictures, making the abstract morph into the concrete. Instead of floating above in a world of abstractions, we are brought back to Earth, finding ourselves surrounded by concrete persons, places, and things.

> *Honesty is an easy word to talk about, but it's harder to put into actual practice. If you pay attention, though, you can see it in action all around you. Honesty is admitting that the fish that got away really wasn't very big anyway. It's making a full stop at a stop sign. It's telling someone how you really feel when they ask: "How's it going?" Honesty is telling the lady at the Department of Motor Vehicles your actual weight or recording your actual score on a golf hole instead of subtracting a stroke. It's telling your teacher the real reason you didn't finish the assignment instead of making up an excuse. It's admitting that the tennis ball was in even though it means you lost the point. It's telling an employee the real reason he's being fired. Honesty is resisting the temptation to glance at your neighbor's test, even though you didn't study and you know that she has all the right answers. Honesty is paying for all the software you have on your computer.*

Lists of specific details tap into common human experience. It's impossible to imagine a reader who wouldn't identify with at least one of these examples. In addition, because they are so specific and familiar in the reader's real world, they tug at a reader's heartstrings, making the reader feel as well as think.

Directions

Select one of the following abstract ideas and define it in concrete terms using lists. Include at least one list using either asyndeton or polysyndeton.

creativity	*curiosity*	*modesty*
compassion	*manners*	*self-confidence*
humility	*diligence*	*self-discipline*
self-reliance	*faith*	*wisdom*
success	*failure*	*anger*

38. CHAMBER OF COMMERCE DESCRIPTION

Directions

The job of a Chamber of Commerce is to present a town in a positive way so that businesses will move there and tourists will visit. Imagine you are writing a description of your hometown or home school for the website of your local Chamber of Commerce. Describe your town in detail, but focus on the positives. Use a little bit of hyperbole (exaggeration, that is) to emphasize what a great place it is, how friendly the people are, and how many exciting things there are to do there. Write at least 200 words, and include at least two lists of particulars in your description. Before you begin writing, brainstorm some lists of details that you might include, such as lists of restaurants, things to do, parks, varieties of people, sights to see, etc.

Picturesque views of lush green hills, snowcapped mountains, sparkling blue waters—this panorama is just one of the many benefits of living in Seattle, Washington. Nestled between Puget Sound and Lake Washington, the Emerald City is not on an island, but sometimes if feels like it.

Fishing and sailing and whale watching and water skiing and scuba diving and rowing are just a few of the activities that Seattleites enjoy in and on the salt waters of Puget Sound and the fresh waters of Lake Washington, Lake Union, and other nearby lakes. Landlubbers also find much to embrace in Seattle, with the rugged Olympic Mountains to the west and the snow-capped peaks of Mount Rainier and the Cascade Mountain range to the east. Camping, golfing, rock-climbing, bicycling, skiing, and hiking are just a small sample of the year-round outdoor activities that Seattle's mild climate offers.

Winters that are not too cold and summers that are just right make Seattle the best-kept secret in the United States. Residents of Seattle love its reputation as a rainy city because it keeps people from moving there; the truth is, however, Seattle is not even in the top ten in annual rainfall among U.S. cities. New York City and nearby Portland, Oregon, both get more rain than Seattle, and yet this lush green paradise on Puget Sound has more things to do and things to see than any other American city.

Chapter 5 Teaching Notes and Answers

33. LISTMANIA

Before giving students the handout, consider opening this activity by creating a classroom list based on a single topic. Here are some possibilities:

> *Daily hassles of being a teenager.*
> *Songs that are probably on my teacher's iPod.*
> *Things that aren't of monetary value but are valuable to me.*
> *Movies that are so terrible that they are memorable.*
> *Songs that would be on the soundtrack of the film of my life story.*

After creating a list of at least fifteen items, pass out the handout, and read the example paragraph on the challenges of being a teen. Point out to students that lists, whether long or short, provide variety and interest for the reader. Below are more examples of effective short lists.

Al Zolynas writes about one magical moment in a restaurant where the music of an accordion player entranced everyone and everything: "For a moment we all floated—the whole restaurant: the patrons, the knives and forks, the wine, the sacrificed fish on plates."

Barbara Ehrenreich, writing in Time magazine, proposes reforming the avarice of the holidays and uses a specific list to remind the reader: "Forget the PlayStations, the Barbie-mobiles, the catalogs and camp-outs in Wal-Mart parking lots."

Next have students compile their own lists. Writing of these lists can be done in small groups, in pairs, or individually. Plan time for students to share some of their lists.

34. ASYNDETON AND POLYSYNDETON

The effect here is subtle, so guide student through the examples and the explanation. These two strategies probably won't be familiar, but once students become aware of them they will probably begin to see them frequently in print. The following are some additional examples that you can use to reinforce the point that writers pay attention to small things, such as whether to insert or delete a conjunction:

> *Asyndeton*
> *Let every nation know, whether it wishes us well or ill, that we shall pay any price, bear any burden, meet any hardships, support any friend, oppose any foe to assure the survival and the success of liberty.*

This classic example is from John F. Kennedy's inaugural address, in which he employs asyndeton to give the listener the impression that America's efforts to defend liberty will know no bounds.

> *Polysyndeton*
> *There's no place out there for graft or greed or lies or compromise with human liberties. —Jimmy Stewart, Mr. Smith Goes to Washington*

Polysyndeton
Tiger Woods, the coolest athlete on Planet Swoosh, has the Swoosh on the front of his hat and the side of his hat and the back of his hat and on his turtleneck and on his shirt and on his sweater and on his vest and on his pants and on his socks and on his shoes. —Rick Reilly

Polysyndeton
Real fatherhood means love and commitment and sacrifice and a willingness to share responsibility and not walking away from one's children.
—William Bennett

Polysyndeton
The tools in my workbench are a double inheritance, for each hammer and level and saw is wrapped in a cloud of knowing. —Scott Russell Sanders

Possible Answers

1. *The rumor spread everywhere in a matter of minutes: to the cafeteria, to the library, to the main office, to the chemistry lab.*
   The rumor spread everywhere in a matter of minutes: to the cafeteria and the library and the main office and the chemistry lab.

2. *His locker was filled to the brim with textbooks, candy wrappers, dirty gym clothes, unfinished homework assignments.*
   His locker was filled to the brim with textbooks and candy wrappers and dirty gym clothes and unfinished homework assignments.

3. *The picture on the television flickers as channels flash by: CNN, ESPN, Discovery Channel.*
   The picture on the television flickers as channels flash by: CNN and ESPN and Discovery Channel.

4. *We will travel to Los Angeles, Chicago, Bismarck, New York.*
   We will travel to Los Angeles and Chicago and Bismarck and New York.

5. *The meal was excellent. We ate T-bone steaks, mashed potatoes, green beans, lemon Jello.*
   The meal was excellent. We ate T-bone steaks and mashed potatoes and green beans and lemon Jello.

35. HYPHENATED MODIFIER

Write one of the example original and revised sentences on the board before handing out the worksheet. Ask students which they prefer. There is no right answer here, but students might notice that the sentence that contains the hyphenated modifier is significantly different than a typical sentence, and significantly more original.

After this brief discussion, give students the handout and introduce the specific details regarding the use of the hyphenated modifier. Make sure to point out that there is no hyphen between the hyphenated modifier and the noun it modifies.

Possible Answers

1. *keep-them-busy-for-at-least-forty-minutes assignment*

2. *I-am-oblivious-to-anyone-else's-needs-but-my-own attitude*

3. *you're-lucky-to-have-a-job looks*

4. *escaped-lunatic-on-Halloween stories*

5. *I-refuse-to-lose-at-any-cost attitude*

6. *I'm-in-love-and-I'm-going-to-make-sure-the-whole-world-knows-it songs*

7. *ninety-minutes-of-car-chases-and-five-minutes-of-dialogue movies*

8. *only-driven-on-Sunday-once-a-month-by-an-eighty-five-year-old-lady car*

36. IN PRAISE OF ...

Pass out the handout and read the example. Ask students to identify how many reasons the writer gives to support his/her love of the Beatles. (They should notice at least twelve.) Also ask students to underline examples of lists and hyphenated modifiers used by the writer to show the point in concrete terms. Before students write their own compositions, ask them to do some pre-writing, listing reasons and lists of details that they might use to show the reader their points.

When students begin to write their drafts, ask them to consider where they might employ asyndeton or polysyndeton for a desired effect. Because students are selecting a topic they care about, plan to allow some time for them to share their passages.

37. DEFINING ABSTRACTIONS

After passing out this handout and reading the example passage about honesty, ask students, "How does the writer of this passage manage to take an abstract idea and show the reader what it looks like in concrete terms?" They will probably notice that the writer uses plenty of examples and concrete nouns that show what honesty looks like in the real world. As students prepare to write their own passages, ask them to select an abstract noun and then list possible images of what the abstract idea looks like in the real world. They can then use these ideas in their composition. If students are struggling, consider doing a whole-class brainstorm using one abstract term; list student ideas on the board so that everyone can see the variety of ways a single idea might be portrayed in concrete terms. Plan time for students to share their final products.

38. CHAMBER OF COMMERCE DESCRIPTION

Before students write their own description, read through the example as a class. Have students identify lists and details that reveal the writer's impressions of Seattle. Then challenge them to use plenty of showing details and lists as they craft their own descriptions.

Figurative Language— Use Compelling Comparisons

OVERVIEW

Unexpected comparisons that create fresh images for the reader form the core of figurative language. With figurative language, the ordinary becomes extraordinary. By applying this important third strategy, students make their ideas come alive for the reader.

The exercises in Chapters 6 through 8 give students many opportunities to practice the four major figurative devices for comparison: simile, personification, metaphor, and allusion. They'll put these devises to good use as they compose full essays in Part II.

PRE- AND POST-POINTS ACTIVITY: SPEAKING FIGURATIVELY

Before introducing students to the activities in Chapter 6–8, you can select one of the 101 topics from the "Resources" section for them to write about.

Use the following example statement to set the stage and explain the exercise. Write the sample question on the board, and create two columns that explore both the positive and negative aspects of the central topic (money) through metaphor and simile; that is, by comparing money to something else.

Question: Is the pursuit of money a virtue or a vice? Explain.

POSITIVE: *MONEY IS LIKE A ...*	NEGATIVE: *MONEY IS LIKE A ...*

If students are having trouble, show them the following examples.

> **Positive:** *Money is like a swift, flowing river current that transports you to your desired destination quickly and with little effort.*

> **Negative:** *Money is like a swift, dangerous river whose jagged rocks can upend your raft at any moment, causing you to drown in its cold, muddy waters.*

After students have completed the activities in Chapters 6–8, have them do this exercise again, using metaphor, simile, personification, or allusion to make their comparisons. Students will notice that these uses of figurative language come much more easily and that their comparisons are much more interesting.

Explain to students that this activity is an excellent pre-writing strategy to use before writing an essay as well as a great way of generating an interesting essay hook for their introductory paragraph. Applying the strategy will be handy in Part II.

CHAPTER 6

Metaphor and Simile— Old Ideas Made New

KEY TERMS

Metaphor: A figurative comparison between two unrelated nouns, such as: *Friendship is a fire that stays aflame only through constant attention.*

Simile: A figurative comparison between two unrelated nouns using *like* or *as*, such as: *Success is like the sunshine—it brings the rattlesnakes out.*

THE WHAT, WHY, AND HOW OF METAPHORS AND SIMILES

Words are legs.
Words are corn.
Words are circus animals.

These three sentences don't make a lot of sense. After all, we all know that words are not legs, not corn, and definitely not circus animals. With a little elaboration, however, a writer can magically turn nonsense into sense:

Words are the legs of the mind; they bear it about, carry it from point to point, bed it down at night, and keep it off the ground and out of the marsh and mists. —Richard Eder

Language is a growing thing that, like a corn crop, has many uses. As a staple, corn feeds people, horses, and hogs; language also serves utilitarian ends. As a colorless liquid, corn intoxicates. So does language, fermented in a sermon, distilled in a song or a story. Corn was made for people, not the other way around. So too with language. —Jim Wayne Miller

Words are as recalcitrant as circus animals, and the unskilled trainer can crack his whip at them in vain. —Gerald Brenan

This is the magic of metaphor in action. Metaphors allow a writer to make connections between two unlike things. Corn is not literally language, but after you read Jim Wayne Miller's metaphor, you understand how he uses corn to illustrate in a concrete, clear, and creative way how words "grow on" us all. No wonder Aristotle, who invented rhetoric, put metaphor at the top of his list of rhetorical devices and declared, "The greatest thing in style is to have a command of metaphor." A metaphor is a figurative comparison between two unrelated nouns. A simile is also a figurative comparison device, except that it uses the words like or as. Metaphorical thinking and writing stretches the mind. Metaphors also invigorate writing and increase the chances that a writer will say something new and fresh.

Good writers don't make the mistake of using a cliché instead of a fresh metaphor. Instead of using a comparison that they have read or heard elsewhere, good writers try their own comparisons. For example, if talking about the importance of friendship, a student might turn to the "bridge over troubled water" cliché. A student who understands the power of metaphors and similes, however, would have options. Instead of the cliché, he might think of something new. How is friendship like a carpet? How is it like a shoe? How is it like a fire?

Example

> *Metaphor: Friendship is a fire that stays aflame only through constant attention.*

> *Simile: Friendship is like a fire that stays aflame only through constant attention.*

Metaphors are powerful because they help the reader to see old ideas in new ways. They are also powerful because they follow the basic writing principle of balancing the abstract and the concrete. For example, in the metaphor above, an abstract idea of friendship is balanced with the concrete idea of fire. The metaphor goes beyond merely telling—it shows by painting a specific picture for the reader.

This chapter will expose students to a variety of examples of metaphors and similes, and it will also explain the essential components that go into making a metaphor and simile. Armed with this knowledge, students will begin applying it by constructing metaphors of their own. In so doing, students will begin to see how metaphors and similes will not only make their writing more interesting, but also open up their imagination to new ways of thinking and new ways of seeing the world.

Chapter 6 Exercises

39. **Metaphorically Speaking.** This activity helps students distinguish between metaphors and similes and supplies a variety of examples that show how great writers craft metaphors to make the abstract concepts concrete.

40. **Creating Fresh Metaphors.** Students craft their own metaphors in this activity.

41. **Explicit and Implicit Metaphors.** Students explore the subtlety and depth of a well-crafted metaphor.

42. **Figurative-language Hook and Full-circle Conclusion.** This activity gives students a valuable strategy to open their essays on a high note and finish with flare.

43. **Commemoration.** This directed writing assignment challenges students to apply metaphors and similes in their own writing.

44. **The Glass Is Half Full.** Students stretch their thinking as they see the power of an extended metaphor.

45. **Life Is a Metaphor.** This fun writing activity helps students to see the limitless possibilities of metaphors, even when writing about a broad, seemingly ordinary topic.

39. METAPHORICALLY SPEAKING

Writers use metaphors and similes to bring abstract ideas to life. Abstract ideas like happiness and advice may exist in our minds, but great writers transform those ideas into concrete pictures by using figurative language to make powerful, fresh comparisons.

Notice how the following metaphor and simile help you see abstract ideas in new ways by comparing them to concrete nouns.

Happiness is not a horse; you cannot harness it. —Chinese proverb

Advice is like snow: The softer it falls, the longer it dwells upon, and the deeper it sinks into, the mind. —Samuel Taylor Coleridge

The first quote is a metaphor: a figurative comparison between two unrelated nouns. The second quote is a simile: a figurative comparison between two unrelated nouns, using "like" or "as."

One of the best ways to learn about metaphors and similes is to read works by professional writers and notice how they use metaphors and similes to make old ideas new. Also notice that for a reader, metaphors and similes make writing more interesting to read.

Directions

For each following quotation, answer three questions. 1.) Is it a metaphor or a simile? 2.) What abstract idea does the metaphor or simile address? 3.) What concrete pictures does the metaphor or simile present to the reader, and how does it help you see the abstract idea in a new way?

1. *Life is a grindstone. Whether it grinds you down or polishes you up depends on what you're made of. —Jacob M. Braude*

2. *Limited vocabulary, like short legs on a pole-vaulter, builds in a natural barrier to progress beyond a certain point. —John Gardner*

3. *The game of life is a game of boomerangs. Our thoughts, deeds, and words return to us sooner or later with astounding accuracy. —Florence Scovel Shinn*

4. *Kindness is the language which the deaf can hear and the blind can see. —Mark Twain*

5. *The past should be culled like a box of fresh strawberries, rinsed of debris, sweetened judiciously, and served in small portions, not very often. —Laura Palmer*

6. *Success is like the sunshine—it brings the rattlesnakes out. —Paul Morton*

7. *Trouble is a sieve through which we sift our acquaintances. Those too big to pass through are our friends. —Arlene Francis*

40. CREATING FRESH METAPHORS

The human mind has an amazing capacity to make connections and to construct metaphors. All you have to do is practice writing them. The following three-step process outlined will help you construct metaphors with ease.

Step 1. Begin with your topic.
Example: Pizza

Step 2. Compare your topic to another unrelated noun, and connect the two topics.
Example: Pizza is a lifesaver.

Step 3. Elaborate on the metaphor by answering who, what, when, where, why, or how.
Example: Pizza is a lifesaver in an ocean of bland food choices; it buoys me up in a sea of crummy cuisine.

Directions

Using the following two columns, follow the three steps for creating a metaphor. Choose a word from Column A for Step 1 and a word from Column B for Step 2. On a separate piece of paper, use at least three different combinations to write three separate complete-sentence metaphors.

Column A	Column B
life	a fish
power	a song
summer	a river
success	a mask
money	a fire
the future	a bird
learning	a knife
imagination	a book
truth	a lunch box
death	an apple
love	a factory

Examples

History is a majestic bird, soaring overhead. People may want to catch and cage it, but they can only look upon it with wonder and respect as it slowly flies away.

Leadership is a knife, slicing cleanly through the chaos.

41. EXPLICIT AND IMPLICIT METAPHORS

Some metaphors are explicit: They identify the major idea or theme being addressed and the comparison. For example, in the metaphor "Anger is the wind that blows out the light of reason," the major theme of the metaphor is "anger," which is being compared to "wind." Because anger is named in the metaphor, it is explicit.

On the other hand, implicit metaphors don't identify the abstract idea or theme being addressed. Instead, they make the comparison and leave it to the reader to interpret the major idea or theme. For example, in the metaphor "Mud thrown is lost ground," the reader must interpret what is being compared with "mud thrown" and "lost ground." With some thought, the reader will realize that this metaphor is about the topic of "name calling."

Another example of an implicit metaphor is, "Many strokes overthrow the tallest oaks." Although the metaphor's topic appears to be about chopping down trees, the larger, implied meaning is the need to persevere, even when a task seems too big to complete.

Directions

Each of the following metaphors is implicit. For each one, first identify the implicit abstract idea or theme addressed in the metaphor, then explain in your own words what the writer is saying about the idea.

Example

> *You can't steal second base and keep your foot on first.*
> *Implicit idea or theme:* success/achievement
> *What the writer is saying about the idea:* Being successful often involves taking risks. Achievers don't stand still; they move forward.

1. *Two men look through the same bars; one sees the mud, and the other sees the stars.*
   Implicit idea or theme:
   What the writer is saying about the idea:

2. *Be a fountain, not a drain.*
   Implicit idea or theme:
   What the writer is saying about the idea:

3. *Anyone can hold the helm when the sea is calm.*
   Implicit idea or theme:
   What the writer is saying about the idea:

4. *People can be induced to swallow anything, provided it is seasoned with praise.*
   Implicit idea or theme:
   What the writer is saying about the idea:

5. *If you want to gather honey, don't kick over the bee hive.*
   Implicit idea or theme:
   What the writer is saying about the idea:

42. FIGURATIVE-LANGUAGE HOOK AND FULL-CIRCLE CONCLUSION

Begin an essay well and the reader's attention is captured; end it well, and the reader feels satisfied. Using figurative language in the very first sentence of a composition is an excellent way to hook your reader. Right away, you create a fresh comparison that takes an abstract idea and transforms it into a concrete image.

A figurative-language hook makes a strong first impression and opens the door for ending your composition with a smooth, satisfying conclusion.

A full-circle conclusion that returns to your opening figure of speech gives your reader the pleasing sense of coming full circle after a successful journey through your essay.

Directions: Read the following passage about the sport of ultimate Frisbee. As you read, notice how the writer employs both a figurative-language hook and a full-circle conclusion:

> Ultimate Frisbee is the antidote to inactivity: a shot in the arm for athletes looking for a cure for common, less active sports. Ultimate is a concentrated flurry of activity that doesn't stop until one team scores. Once this happens, the teams get a short break, but seconds later they get right back to playing—no time for bench warming, time outs, or extended halftimes. The fast and furious games can go on for two hours, so players need a lot of endurance to play effectively. Ultimate athletes need the agility of a cat because they are constantly diving and jumping and rolling around to block the disk, catch the disk, or just keep up with everyone else. It's great training for other sports such as basketball, baseball, or soccer—which seem tame and sedentary by comparison. Ultimate players need excellent eye-hand coordination, but they must also be able to run for a long time, usually sprinting. In addition, they must know where the disk is at all times and be able to adjust their actions according to that position. No placebo, ultimate Frisbee is just what the doctor ordered for athletes looking for a sport that develops finesse, fosters fitness, and features non-stop fun.

1. What figure of speech does the writer use in the first sentence?

2. What metaphor does the writer refer to in the concluding sentence to bring the reader full circle?

3. As a reader, how would you describe the effect of the writer's use of a figurative-language hook and a full-circle conclusion?

4. Now select your own topic from the list your teacher supplies. Write an introductory paragraph where you address the question using a figurative language hook.

43. COMMEMORATION

What specific event or date on the calendar should be commemorated? Try for events or dates that aren't already commemorated.

Examples

A historic event (such as Custer's Last Stand or the invention of the Post-It Note)

A landmark anniversary (The World Cow Chip Throwing Championship or the Roswell UFO Incident)

An important birthday (Shakespeare or Harry Potter)

Directions

Pick an event like the ones above. Explain why the event is important to commemorate. Write at least 150 words, using at least one or more metaphors or similes to persuade the reader that your date is important.

Notice how the following example uses metaphors to talk about the influence of Galileo.

History teaches us that about once every millennium an individual life shines so brightly that it illuminates the future, long after that life is over. One such life was that of Galileo Galilei, who died on January 8, 1642, in Italy. Forced into seclusion at the end of his life by the Catholic Church, which saw his ideas as heresy, Galileo might have died in obscurity. However, the bright shining light of his ideas could not be extinguished. An astronomer, physicist, and mathematician, Galileo's ideas gave birth to modern science. His construction of the first astronomical telescope, his explanation of the laws of motion, and his development of the scientific method are just a small sample of his contributions to human learning. He died a blind man, under house arrest, but his spirit lives on to inspire free thought and to help us to see the power of scientific thinking. We should honor every January 8th as Galileo Day, remembering that great minds live on, their brilliance and genius lighting the path to future discoveries in science.

44. THE GLASS IS HALF FULL

Read the following paragraph, and notice how it uses the metaphor of a river to talk about music.

> *I am most optimistic about music. Music is a river of unlimited depth and breadth that winds through every life. We can sit on its grassy banks, enjoying the soothing sounds of its flowing rapids, or we can jump into its cool waters and become a part of its relentless flow. This river takes us to places we have never been before, and whether we dive deep into its depths or glide gently on its serene surface, it nourishes our spirit and buoys our imagination. This river is ancient, and yet it is constantly changing, and each time we come to it we experience something new and something beautiful.*

You might have noticed that in addition to mentioning a river, the passage also uses other words associated with a river that extend the metaphor and elaborate on the comparisons between the abstract idea of music and the concrete idea of a river. Words like depth, breadth, rapids, buoys, flow, surface, dive, and grassy banks extend the connections between music and a river, helping us to not only understand the writer's point, but also to exercise our powers of imagination to see it in our mind's eye in concrete terms.

Directions

What single thing are you most optimistic about? Why? Explain the what and the why of your optimism in at least 100 words; include one or more metaphors or similes.

I. Before you begin writing, use the following three steps to focus your thinking.

STEP 1	STEP 2	STEP 3
Begin by identifying your topic, the single thing you are most optimistic about.	Decide what you want to compare it to.	Brainstorm a list of words that you associate with this thing. For example, if you are comparing your topic to a book, you might list: *pages, margin, cover, binding, words, loaning, buying, reading aloud, summarizing.*

II. As you write your paragraph, focus on making specific comparisons that give your reader concrete pictures that illustrate why you are so optimistic about your topic.

45. LIFE IS A METAPHOR

Metaphors help us see even the everyday, ordinary parts of our world in fresh ways. What could be more everyday and ordinary than the topic "life"? Notice how the following examples compare life to a grindstone, a zoo, a melody, and a fire:

> *Life is a grindstone. Whether it grinds us down or polishes us up depends on us.* —*Thomas L. Holdcroft*

> *Life is a zoo in a jungle.* —*Peter De Vries*

> *Life is a melody that you can sing by yourself, but it is often more beautiful when someone comes along to harmonize.*

> *Life is a bright, dancing fire that is never meant to be still for even a moment.*

Directions

Finish each of the following stems explaining and elaborating on the connection between the two nouns. Select your best one. Revise it and then share it with someone.

Life is a train … _____

Life is a book … _____

Life is a ladder … _____

Life is a tree … _____

Life is a computer … _____

Life is a rope … _____

Life is a stone … _____

Life is a wave … _____

Life is a wind … _____

Life is an apple … _____

Revised metaphor: _____

_____

_____

39. METAPHORICALLY SPEAKING

Before passing out the worksheet, show students some of the following quotes.

1. *Be like a postage stamp—stick to one thing until you get there. —Josh Billings*
2. *Debt is a trap which man sets and baits himself, and then deliberately gets into. —Josh Billings*
3. *Trying to sneak a pitch past him is like trying to sneak the sunrise past a rooster. —Amos Otis about Rod Carew, Hall of Fame first baseman.*
4. *Time is a storm in which we are all lost. —Napoleon Bonaparte*
5. *Time is a file that wears and makes no noise. —English proverb*
6. *Baseball games are like snowflakes and fingerprints, no two are ever alike. —W.P. Kinsella*
7. *Don't tell me how rough the waters are. Just bring the ship in. —Chuck Knox*
8. *When you get to the end of your rope, tie a knot and hang on. —Franklin D. Roosevelt*
9. *Fortune is like the market, where many times, if you can stay a little, the price will fall. —Francis Bacon*

Then ask them if they notice what these sentences have in common. Students should notice that they all use language in a non-literal way; in other words, the writers are using metaphors. Next, pass out the handout, which gives definitions and explanations of how writers use metaphors. Since this is the first lesson on figurative language, guide students through the first few examples and problems.

Possible Answers

1. Metaphor; life; grindstone: The reader can visualize the two uses of the grindstone.

2. Simile; vocabulary; short legs: The reader can visualize a successful or unsuccessful pole-vaulter.

3. Metaphor; life; boomerang: The reader can visualize the flight of a boomerang.

4. Metaphor; kindness; language: The reader can relate to written and spoken language.

5. Simile; the past; strawberries: The reader can visualize the process of rinsing strawberries.

6. Simile; success; sunshine: The reader can visualize the rattlesnake basking in the sun.

7. Metaphor; trouble; a sieve: The reader can visualize the process of sifting with a sieve.

40. CREATING FRESH METAPHORS

Guide students through the three-step process, making sure they follow each step. Use the pizza example to demonstrate. For the first metaphor students create, you could assign a random word from Column A and Column B and ask them to combine the two into a metaphor. This demonstrates that the imaginative human mind can combine virtually any two ideas to create a fresh metaphor. As students compose their metaphors, have them share examples with partners, small groups, or with the whole class. My students and I have been astounded by the fresh comparisons and images that result from this activity.

Possible Answers

The future is a shark that relentlessly pursues and devours its prey: the past.

Summer is a sweet, but short, song that is sung by children with filthy knees and smiling faces.

Money is a dull knife that cuts to the bone.

41. EXPLICIT AND IMPLICIT METAPHORS

This lesson helps students see the way figurative language often challenges the reader to interpret implied meaning. Guide students through this handout, emphasizing that there is no single right answer. However, they should be able to logically defend their answers based on the words in each metaphor.

Possible Answers

1. Implicit idea or theme: attitude
   What the writer is saying about the idea: A person's attitude influences the way he/she sees the world.

2. Implicit idea or theme: attitude
   What the writer is saying about the idea: We have a choice to contribute positively to our world or to be a negative influence.

3. Implicit idea or theme: fortitude/perseverance
   What the writer is saying about the idea: Difficult circumstances test a person's real character.

4. Implicit idea or theme: persuasion/influence
   What the writer is saying about the idea: People are predisposed to believe someone who offers them praise.

5. Implicit idea or theme: success
   What the writer is saying about the idea: Pursue positive outcomes through positive, productive actions.

42. FIGURATIVE-LANGUAGE HOOK AND FULL-CIRCLE CONCLUSION

Emphasize in this activity that using figurative language as a hook is a powerful way to capture the reader's attention; it just about guarantees that you will say something original. Before students write their own paragraphs, read the example about optimism and discuss the questions that follow as a class.

Answers

1. The writer uses a metaphor.
2. The writer refers to a pill, which relates back to the "antidote" in the first sentence.
3. The metaphor helps the reader see the abstract idea of optimism in a more concrete way, as a powerful, helpful medicine.

43. COMMEMORATION

Before students write their own compositions, read the example passage about Galileo. Ask them, "How does the writer's use of figurative language in this passage help the reader see the writer's point?" Students should notice the multiple uses of light as a metaphor for Galileo's "brilliance." Have them circle the different words associated with light so that they can see the way the writer weaves the metaphor throughout the passage.

Next, challenge students to write about an event or anniversary they feel is important or worthwhile, selecting a single metaphor to bring it to life for the reader. Plan time for students to share their final pieces.

44. THE GLASS IS HALF FULL

Read aloud the example passage on music. Ask students to highlight the words the writer uses to extend the river metaphor, and emphasize that these words are words that have associations with a river. As students work on the assignment to create their own compositions, highlight the importance of Step 3. Try to get them to list at least ten associations; they may not eventually use them all, but making the associations will extend their imaginations. Discourage students from writing until they have completed all three steps.

45. LIFE IS A METAPHOR

Students can share their life metaphors in pairs, small groups, or with the whole class. It is important to see the different ways a single comparison like a "ladder" or a "train" can be used to create completely different images and attitudes by different writers.

Here are three examples that use the "life is a ladder" metaphor:

Life is a ladder with five broken rungs.

Life is 50-foot ladder secured to the ground by family, friendship, and faith.

Life is a ladder that we construct one rung at a time, using whatever materials chance happens to throw our way.

Chapter 6 Metaphor and Simile—Old Ideas Made New

CHAPTER **7**

Personification—It's Alive

THE WHAT, WHY, AND HOW OF PERSONIFICATION

The English language is alive, and he's hungry—hungry for new words that is. He doesn't discriminate: He collects words from computer geeks as well as gang-bangers, soccer moms as well as deadbeat dads. He's a world traveler who has been spending a lot of time in China recently. He's a fan of the Internet, and he sends several text messages every day; one of his favorite places, though, is hanging out by the water cooler listening to conversations. He loves to share words, but also does his share of borrowing. Just when you think you've got him pegged, he changes, adding new meanings and new connotations to his wardrobe of words. He loves his freedom, and laughs out loud when English teachers tell him what he is supposed to be like. He just shrugs his shoulders, gives you a sly wink, and unexpectedly changes a noun into a verb.

What if you had the power to breathe life into inanimate objects? What if you could put arms and legs on an abstract idea, watch it walk around the room, and then teach it to talk? In the world of writing, these are not "ifs," they are realities. Personification is the rhetorical device the writer uses to describe objects, animals, or ideas using human characteristics. The passage about the English language that opens this chapter is an excellent example of the powerful effect that personification can have on the reader. An abstract idea like language comes alive by giving it human characteristics and human motion: it loves, it laughs, it sends text messages, and it shrugs its shoulders.

Because it employs vivid verbs, concrete nouns, and specific adjectives, personification boasts one of the fundamental features of good writing: specific, detailed word choice. The added benefit of personification, however, is figurative language. It allows the writer to show similarity in the dissimilar, to make fresh comparisons, and to create vivid, lively images.

One final advantage of personification is that it allows students, no matter what they are writing about, to write about their reader's favorite topic: people.

The exercises and activities in this chapter allow students to not only understand personification, but also see it in action. They'll learn how it enlivens writing in more ways than one, and they will learn to apply it by using specific word choice.

Chapter 7 Exercises

46. **Personification: Bring Words to Life.** This exercise introduces students to multiple examples of personification and encourages them to analyze the technique.

47. **Personification in Practice.** Students use personification as they write their own sentences.

48. **Abstractions in the Flesh.** Students see how personification can transform an idea into a living, breathing person.

49. **Time Flies.** Students apply personification to a topic they feel strongly about, either negatively or positively.

50. **Make Your Toothpaste Sing.** This writing activity allows students to apply personification to the persuasive language of advertising.

51. **I Am the Textbook, I Make You Work.** In this fun writing activity, students apply personification while experimenting with point of view.

46. PERSONIFICATION: BRING WORDS TO LIFE

In the following passage, the writer talks about trees. Notice how the writer uses words that are normally reserved for people to describe trees.

> *Human beings grew up in forests; we have a natural affinity for them. How lovely a tree is, straining toward the sky. Its leaves harvest sunlight to photosynthesize, so trees compete by shadowing their neighbors. If you look closely you can often see two trees pushing and shoving with languid grace.*
> —Carl Sagan from *Cosmos*

Personification is the rhetorical device by which the writer describes objects, animals, or ideas using human characteristics. The previous passage about trees is an excellent example of the powerful effect personification can have on the reader. A non-human subject becomes human: trees *strain*, they *compete*, they *push*, they *shove*.

The simple secret of personification is selecting the right words to animate the inanimate. To personify, use words normally used to describe people to describe ideas or things. Use adjectives like *thoughtful* or *honest*; use verbs like *smile* or *sings*; use concrete nouns like *hands* or *feet*; or use pronouns like *he* or *they*.

Directions

Read the following examples of personification carefully. As you read, first circle the specific words that bring life to the non-human topics discussed in each quote. Then extend the personification by adding at least four words or an additional sentence.

Example

> *Oreo: Milk's favorite cookie, fun's favorite midnight snack.*
> —Cookie advertisement

1. *He that hath wife and children hath given hostages to fortune.* —Francis Bacon

2. *There is no armor against fate; death lays his icy hands on kings.* —Jane Shirley

3. *The road isn't built that can make it breathe hard!* —Advertisement for Chevrolet

4. *Happiness hates the timid.* —Eugene O'Neill

5. *The only monster here is the gambling monster that has enslaved your mother! I call him Gamblor, and it's time to snatch your mother from his neon claws!* —Homer Simpson

6. *Wisdom never kicks at the iron walls it can't bring down.* —Olive Schreiner

7. *Nature, to be commanded, must be obeyed.* —Francis Bacon

8. *Time is the wisest counselor.* —Pericles

47. PERSONIFICATION IN PRACTICE

Because it employs vivid verbs, concrete nouns, and specific adjectives, personification boasts one of the fundamental features of good writing: specific, detailed word choice. Because it is a figurative device for comparison, it allows the writer to show similarity in the dissimilar, to make fresh comparisons, and to create vivid, lively images.

One final advantage of personification is that it allows you—no matter what you are writing about—to write about the reader's favorite topic: people.

Directions

Re-write the following sentences using personification to make the literal sentences figurative.

> *Original: The sun rose.*
>
> *Revised: The sun was tardy, sluggishly climbing from behind the mountains, making no excuses for its lateness.*

1. *It rained hard last night.*

2. *Love is difficult.*

3. *The textbook was heavy.*

4. *We can learn from our mistakes.*

5. *The television was too loud.*

48. ABSTRACTIONS IN THE FLESH

Personification is a great way to turn the abstract into the concrete. Take an abstract idea, such as success or failure, and use personification to give it arms and legs and to describe it in action, as though you're describing a quirky next-door neighbor or a good friend. In the following example, notice how nouns, adjectives, verbs, and personal pronouns are used to give life to the abstract idea of "humor."

> *Humor is unpredictable. He hides around corners and jumps out when you least expect him. He's optimistic, healthy, and smart. Never depressing or anxious, he thrives on the unsuspected and spontaneous. He's a great companion, constantly reminding you to loosen up, look at the bright side, and smile more often. He loves to break up fights—when he's around no one has the strength to make a fist.*

Directions

Take an abstract quality, like the following ones listed, and describe it in action using personification. Write at least sixty words.

intelligence	stupidity	success	failure	truth
victory	defeat	the past	the future	technology
diligence	procrastination	war	peace	imagination
power	poverty	education	loyalty	tradition

49. TIME FLIES

Directions

What is your favorite or least favorite season of the year, month of the year, or day of the week? Explain what you like or dislike about it, and use personification to enhance your description and explanation. Write at least eighty words, and try to use words that reveal your attitude (either positive or negative) toward your topic.

Notice, for example, how the following paragraph uses personification.

> *Monday stands menacingly over you as you sleep on Sunday night. He breathes heavily, and his breathe stinks. When morning arrives, he rings a loud, ear-shattering bell that jolts you awake. Dazed and disoriented, you eventually deduce that another workweek lies ahead. As you get up and get ready, Monday mocks you, smirking, pointing at you, and laughing hysterically. As you race out the front door, Monday kicks you in the butt, yells sarcastically, "Have a great day, sucker!!" and slams the door behind you.*

50. MAKE YOUR TOOTHPASTE SING

Directions

Write the text of a radio advertisement of at least fifty words in which you personify an inanimate product to make it more appealing to the buyer.

Example

Flanders Coffee's inviting aroma and rich taste are your daily wake-up call, not from a stranger, but from a trusted, benevolent neighbor who sets the tone for your day, saying: "Good morning, friend, you look wide awake, alert, energetic, and ready to take on your day!" Why wouldn't you be? Flanders Coffee—it's like having a friendly neighbor watching out for you!

51. I AM THE TEXTBOOK, I MAKE YOU WORK

In one of his most well-known poems, American poet Carl Sandburg personifies grass. He does more than give it arms and legs, though; he gives it a voice and a job to do. In the poem, appropriately titled "Grass," the grass describes in first person how it has worked throughout time, covering up fallen soldiers on various battlefields throughout history.

> *Pile the bodies high at Austerlitz and Waterloo.*
> *Shovel them under and let me work—*
> *I am the grass; I cover all.*

Directions

Select your own non-human object and give it a voice, writing at least 100 words. Imagine what it would say and what it would say about its job. Your tone may be serious or silly.

> *computer*
> *textbook*
> *coffee cup*
> *paper clip*
> *notebook*
> *tennis racket*
> *alarm clock*
> *cell phone*
> *musical instrument*
> *bicycle*

Example

> *People take me for granted, saying: "You're just a common, everyday No. 2 pencil." They don't realize that I'm quite cosmopolitan. My lead is a combination of graphite from Mexico and Sri Lanka, mixed with Mississippi mud. My eraser blends South American rubber and Italian pumice, and my shaft is made of California cedar. So, as you can see I'm not your ordinary, run-of-the-mill school supply. I've been places and seen things, and you can trust that I'll help you get your most important ideas down on paper.*

Chapter 7 Teaching Notes and Answers

46. PERSONIFICATION: BRING WORDS TO LIFE

Before giving students the handout, you can use the following quote
to illustrate personification.

> [H]istory made bur oak the characteristic tree of the southern Wisconsin when
> the prairie grasses first gained possession of the region. Bur oak is the only tree
> that can stand up to a prairie fire and live… This cork is armor. Bur oaks were
> the shock troops sent by the invading forest to storm the prairie; fire is what
> they had to fight.
> —Aldo Leopold

The following are examples of words normally reserved for describing people. When
writers use these words to describe anything other than people, however, the ideas
or the things come to life.

Words for Personification

Adjectives	Action Verbs	Concrete Nouns	Personal Pronouns
thoughtful	smiles	feet	he
honest	winks	hands	she
mean	remembers	color	his
caring	sleeps	heart	her
courageous	mumbles	eyes	their
loyal	sings	fingers	they

The handout contains another example along with explanation. Since this is the
students' introduction to personification, guide them through the assignment, making
sure they see the words that signal the personification. Seeing these words will help
them as they expand the quotes with their own ideas.

Possible Answers

1. *He that hath wife and children hath given hostages to fortune, and awaits
   a ransom note written in blood. —Francis Bacon*
2. *There is no armor against fate; death lays his icy hands on kings and his
   clutching grip on presidents. —Jane Shirley*
3. *The road isn't built that can make it breathe hard! No known mountain can make
   its pulse quicken. —Advertisement for Chevrolet*
4. *Happiness hates the timid. He befriends the bold. —Eugene O'Neill*
5. *The only monster here is the gambling monster that has enslaved your mother!
   I call him Gamblor, and it's time to snatch your mother from his neon claws! He
   lurks at night in back alleys and feasts on the flesh of the weak. —Homer Simpson*
6. *Wisdom never kicks at the iron walls it can't bring down. She knows when
   to submit and when to fight. —Olive Schreiner*
7. *Nature, to be commanded, must be obeyed. She's loving but demanding, gentle
   but powerful. —Francis Bacon*
8. *Time is the wisest counselor. His lessons, however, are not free. —Pericles*

47. PERSONIFICATION IN PRACTICE

Before giving students the handout for this activity, show them the paragraph on the English language that opens this chapter. Ask them: "How does the writer's use of personification make this a more interesting passage than if the writer had used literal language?" There is no single right answer to this question, but students should see that personification does enliven the passage for the reader as it provides more images and movement. As you pass out the handout, tell students that they will have an opportunity to try their own hands at transforming a literal sentence into a figurative one using personification.

Possible Answers

1. *The rain slammed against our windows, door, and roof last night, trying to keep us awake.*

2. *Love never allows you to take the easy route; he's always putting up detours, "wrong way" signs, and roadblocks.*

3. *The textbook sat at the bottom of my backpack, pulling me forcefully to the ground.*

4. *Mistakes are benevolent teachers who offer us helpful lessons.*

5. *The television's blaring, barking voice crushed our eardrums.*

48. ABSTRACTION IN THE FLESH

Before students write about their own abstract idea using personification, read the example paragraph about humor as a class. Ask students: "How does the writer use personification to bring this abstract idea to life?" Remind students of the key words (nouns, adjectives, verbs, and pronouns) that must be used with personification. Prompt them with questions like, "If imagination walked into this room, what is the first thing it would do?" or "If war was a person, what clothes would he or she wear?" Students can use these questions to jot down ideas before writing their complete passage.

49. TIME FLIES

Before students write their own compositions, read through the example passage in which Monday is personified. Ask students how the writer's use of personification makes an everyday topic such as Monday stand out. Point out that whether they write about a favorite or least favorite topic, their word choice should reveal their attitude to the reader. In the Monday paragraph, for example, words like menacingly, ear-shattering, and mocks reveal that the writer has a negative attitude toward Monday. Allow time in class for students to share their passages so that they can hear the contrasting ideas and attitudes.

50. MAKE YOUR TOOTHPASTE SING

As you pass out the handout for this activity, read the example coffee advertisement. Ask students for examples of products that might be advertised on the radio and list them on the board. Make sure to set aside time for students to read their ads aloud so that student can hear the full effect. You might even consider having students record them, adding music and sound effects as appropriate.

51. I AM THE TEXTBOOK, I MAKE YOU WORK

Before passing out the handout, consider reading students the entire poem "Grass" by Carl Sandburg. (It is a much anthologized poem and should be easy to find on the Internet.) Ask students what is being personified in the poem and what the poet is saying about the topic of war. Students should be able to identify the voice of the grass talking about its "job" throughout the centuries: covering the dead bodies of soldiers killed in battle. Next, pass out the handout and read the example passage on the No. 2 pencil. Ask students how this passage is similar to "Grass." They will probably notice that both passages feature not only personification, but also the voice of the personified object. This discussion will prepare students to select their own topics to personify and give voice to. Allow time for students to share their final products, either in small groups or with the entire class.

CHAPTER 8

Allusions—Name Dropping

> ### KEY TERMS
>
> **Allusion:** A reference to a person, place, or thing from history, mythology, or literature.

THE WHAT, WHY, AND HOW OF ALLUSIONS

> *Tofu. The Holy Grail of foods. The Mecca of meals. Sound a bit much? What some see as just coagulated soy milk, the enlightened view as quintessential culinary magic. The Proteus of the culinary world, tofu earns an A+ because of its versatility and adaptability. It can be used in stir fries, grilled foods, dips, salad dressings, soups, shakes, smoothies, and desserts. There are tofu burgers, tofu quiche, tofu rice salad, tofu sloppy joes, tofu ravioli, and tofu chocolate cake. Also nutritious, it can provide up to 20 percent of your daily calcium needs and is high in protein and low in fat. It's also an excellent source of iron and B vitamins. With so many menu possibilities and tasty choices, no wonder some people call it "the food of the gods."*

How can you tell a story using only one word? In the paragraph above, the writer employs three allusions—Holy Grail, Mecca, and Proteus—to complement the positive tone of the paragraph. The writer assumes the audience will recognize the allusions; in other words, the story behind the object known as the Holy Grail, the place called Mecca, and the person named Proteus. The writer also trusts that the reader is able to see the figurative comparison between these stories and the writer's point.

Hiroshima, Hercules, Hamlet, and Holocaust—each of these proper nouns conjures up a story from history, mythology, or literature. In addition to referring to a story, each word relays a universal theme, such as destruction, strength, indecision, or death. When writers use allusions, they make connections and associations between these stories and themes, and their topic. With allusions, the proper noun becomes a metaphor; the back story figuratively amplifies the idea being discussed.

Learning to use allusions will help students make connections between what they are writing and a larger historical and cultural context. Allusions show students that they are not writing in a vacuum. Instead, they can draw upon a rich array of past stories to illuminate their points.

The activities that follow introduce students to allusions, help them see how an allusion can enliven a sentence and give it a deeper meaning, and provide valuable practice integrating allusions into their own writing.

Teaching note: Because some of your students may not be familiar with some of the allusions from this chapter, consider giving students the handout, "Allusion Back Stories" at the end of this chapter. You might list some of the allusions on the board before giving students the handout. Ask them how many of the names they recognize. Then, when students get the handout, have them check to verify which names they knew and which they didn't.

Chapter 8 Exercises

52. **What's in a Name?** This activity will help students understand the two key components of an allusion: a story and an idea.

53. **Allusions: From Story to Idea.** Students gain practice recognizing the ideas that allusions evoke.

54. **Speaking Figuratively.** Students begin applying allusions in their own writing.

55. **Grade A Allusions.** Students practice using allusions while writing about a topic they are enthusiastic about.

56. **Cell Phones.** Students apply allusions while expressing their opinion on a given topic.

57. **Allusion Meets Advertising.** In this fun writing activity, students experiment with allusions and point of view.

52. WHAT'S IN A NAME?

How can you tell a story with only one word? Using allusions, writers refer to names of people, places, and events from history, mythology, or literature. They do this to conjure up the story behind the name in the mind of the reader, making a connection between the story and the idea that they are writing about.

With allusions, you aren't just writing in a vacuum. Instead, you connect your ideas to a larger historical and cultural context. The word, in effect, becomes a symbol for the entire story it represents. Notice how in the following quote, Ray Bradbury connects allusions from mythology to his discussion of television.

> The television, that insidious beast, that Medusa which freezes a billion people to stone every night, staring fixedly, that Siren which called and sang and promised so much and gave, after all, so little. —Ray Bradbury

More than just telling us that television is dangerous, Bradbury shows us by alluding to dangerous women from mythology, women whose threatening, fearful associations help the reader make connections and better see Bradbury's point. Bradbury's allusions also bring variety, energy, and interest to the sentence. By conjuring these stories he is expressing an old idea in a new, fresh way.

Directions

See if you can make the connection between the writer's topic and the writer's allusion in the following quotes.

1. *Language is the Rubicon that divides man from beast. —Max Muller*

   Idea: _____

   Story: _____

2. *Discipline prevailed: in five minutes the confused throng was resolved into order, and comparative silence quelled the Babel clamor of tongues. —Charlotte Bronte*

   Idea: _____

   Story: _____

3. *Conversion for me was not a Damascus Road experience. I slowly moved into an intellectual acceptance of what my intuition had always known. —Madeleine L'Engle*

   Idea: _____

   Story: _____

4. *The proposed nuclear deal with India is just one more step in opening a Pandora's Box of nuclear proliferation. —Jimmy Carter*

   Idea: _____

   Story: _____

53. ALLUSIONS: FROM STORY TO IDEA

Allusions pack the powerful combination of stories and ideas. When you use an allusion, you are invoking both a story and the ideas that relate to it. Like a metaphor, using an allusion will amplify your ideas by conjuring up specific images in the mind of your reader. These images will help you go beyond just telling; they will help you show as well.

Directions

See if you can match up each of the following ten allusions with the idea that the story of the person, place, or thing represents.

1. Watergate
2. Sisyphus
3. Sour grapes
4. Big Brother
5. Eden
6. Walter Mitty
7. Prometheus
8. Luddites
9. Catch-22
10. Judas

A. _____ Endless, fruitless labor

B. _____ Lonely and valiant resistance to authority

C. _____ Focusing on the use of the imagination and daydreaming

D. _____ Betrayal by a supposed friend

E. _____ Political scandal

F. _____ Resistance to change/progress

G. _____ Resentment based on an inability to obtain something

H. _____ A double bind or lose-lose situation

I. _____ An all-seeing tyrannical government

J. _____ A paradise of perfect happiness

54. SPEAKING FIGURATIVELY

Notice the difference in the following two sentences.

> *With his backpack full of heavy textbooks, Bill climbed his steep driveway.*

> *Bill was Sisyphus, climbing his steep driveway every day, backpack full of heavy textbooks.*

If you know the story from Greek mythology about Sisyphus, who is sentenced by the gods to roll a huge stone up a hill for eternity, the second sentence probably creates a more vivid image in your mind—an image that might also include the ideas of effort, strain, and futile labor. This is the power of allusions to transform a mundane sentence into a magnificent one.

Directions

Write four sentences, and in each sentence figuratively use at least one of the following allusions. If an allusion is unfamiliar to you, read the "Allusion Back Stories" your teacher has given you.

> *Icarus*
> *The Tower of Babel*
> *Gordian knot*
> *Antaeus*
> *Don Quixote*
> *El Dorado*
> *Pontius Pilate*
> *Pyrrhic victory*
> *Cinderella*

1. _____

2. _____

3. _____

4. _____

55. GRADE A ALLUSIONS

Read the following passage, and see whether you recognize the allusions made by the writer:

> *Tofu. The Holy Grail of foods. The Mecca of meals. Sound a bit much? What some see as just coagulated soy milk in block form, the enlightened gourmets call quintessential culinary magic. As one of the wonders of the food world, tofu earns an A+ because of its versatility and adaptability. Tofu makes appearances in stir-fries, grilled foods, dips, salad dressings, soups, shakes, smoothies, and desserts. There are tofu burgers, tofu quiche, tofu rice salad, tofu sloppy joes, tofu ravioli, and even tofu chocolate cake. It's nutritious, too, as it is high in protein, low in fat, and provides up to 20 percent of your daily calcium needs. It's also an excellent source of iron and B vitamins. For all the many tasty and nutritious menu possibilities of this magical, mutable food, it's no wonder that some people call it "the Proteus of all foods."*

Note that the writer employs three allusions—Holy Grail, Mecca, and Proteus—to complement the positive tone. The writer assumes the audience will recognize the allusions, in other words, the story behind the object known as the Holy Grail, the religious destination known as Mecca, and the Greek god Proteus. The writer also trusts that the reader is able to see the figurative comparison between these stories and the writer's point about tofu.

Directions

Write at least 100 words evaluating something by giving it a specific grade (claim) supported by at least one specific criterion (a premise). Your thesis should state a specific letter grade or evaluative adjective. In addition, you should support your thesis with specific criteria by which the topic is judged.

Examples

> *Under the category of best musical groups of all time, the Beatles earn an A because of their lasting influence.*

> *The Proteus of the culinary world, tofu earns an A+ because of its versatility and adaptability.*

Include in your evaluation at least one allusion to help convey your attitude toward the topic you are evaluating.

56. CELL PHONES

Directions

What statement would you make either positively or negatively about cell phones? Make your statement in at least 100 words, and support it with evidence, examples, explanation, and full-circle conclusion. Also, include at least one allusion that conveys your attitude toward cell phones. This one includes a reference to the irresistible lure of the sirens found in *The Odyssey* by Homer.

Example

Everywhere I go, I see people blindly stumbling in the direction of the Siren song of the cell phone. In their cars, on the sidewalk, in line at the grocery store, they become oblivious to the world around them and instead gaze expectantly at their cell phones.

You know the type of people I'm talking about. There's the I-actually-made-a-conscious-decision-to-choose-"Who-Let-the-Dogs-Out"-as-my-ringtone guy whose cell phone barks at everyone who is trapped with him in the elevator. There's the woman who has the gall not just to answer her cell at the jazz concert, but to also carry on a ten-minute conversation, without whispering, as you try to enjoy the music.

When will these people wake up, open their eyes, and end this cell phone insanity?

_____

_____

_____

_____

_____

_____

_____

_____

_____

_____

57. ALLUSION MEETS ADVERTISING

Directions

Write the text of a radio advertisement of at least 100 words in which a famous character from literature or a famous person from history advertises a product. Based on the person/character's background and history, what would he/she sell today, and what would he/she say to sell the product?

Use one of the following ideas or one of your own.

> *Shakespeare selling a spell-checker*
> *Columbus selling a GPS system*
> *Alexander Graham Bell selling a cell phone*
> *Romeo and Juliet promoting an online dating service*
> *Hercules selling a cleaning product*
> *Albert Einstein selling a hair-care product*
> *Cinderella selling shoes*
> *Abraham Lincoln selling an electric shaver*
> *Beethoven selling an iPod*

Example

People often blame me for opening that box that released all of life's misery and sin. Truth is, it wasn't my fault. Instead, it was that shoddy suitcase Zeus gave me, made of cheap material with a substandard lock. As you can imagine, it was a heavy bag. When I set it down, it sprang open like a jack-in-the-box. Oops! Well, I learned my lesson. From now on, I travel only with the highest quality luggage: Carbonite. Take it from me, Pandora. Think out of the box and get your own Carbonite luggage today.

_____

_____

_____

_____

_____

_____

_____

_____

_____

Chapter 8 Teaching Notes and Answers

52. WHAT'S IN A NAME?

Before giving students the handout, write one or both of the following quotes on the board.

> *Few tasks are more like the torture of Sisyphus than housework, with its endless repetition: the clean becomes soiled, the soiled is made clean, over and over, day after day.* —Simone de Beauvoir

> *Foreign correspondents were a revered, much romanticized group—the Indiana Joneses of journalism.* —The New Yorker, 1995

Ask students if they can explain how the proper nouns in either sentence relate to the writer's point. Students will probably recognize the adventurous Indiana Jones, but they may not recognize Sisyphus, the rock-rolling character from Greek mythology. If you have given students the list of "Allusion Back Stories," they can use it for reference. The key point here is that both writers have used the proper noun as a way to evoke a story that relates to the sentence's point. One story (Sisyphus) is about fruitless effort; the second (Indiana Jones) is about adventure. Next, pass out the handout and guide students through the Ray Bradbury quote and accompanying explanation of how writers use allusions. Finally, have students try to identify the ideas and stories behind the quotations.

53. ALLUSIONS: FROM STORY TO IDEA

Allusions are a form of cultural shorthand that pack the dramatic power of a story into one word.

If you have given students the list of "Allusion Back Stories," have them put it away as they complete this activity. See whether they can match the ten allusions with the ten themes without looking at the list. You might go through the answers, asking students to explain not just the answers, but also the connections between the themes and the stories behind the allusions. See "Allusion Back Stories" for the story.

1. *Idea: An audacious or vitally important act.*
2. *Idea: Confusion, especially in language or communication.*
3. *Idea: A life-changing event or epiphany.*
4. *Idea: Unleashing of uncontrollable and unintended negative consequences.*

Answers

A.	2	**F.**	8
B.	7	**G.**	3
C.	6	**H.**	9
D.	10	**I.**	4
E.	1	**J.**	5

54. SPEAKING FIGURATIVELY

Before students write their sentences in this activity, remind them that the theme behind the allusion/story should be their focus. To get ideas, they should begin with the theme and then apply it to a modern situation. For example, a theme in the story of Icarus is disobedience or reckless audacity. Using this theme, a student might write the following sentence: "Like Icarus, Bill ignored his father's instructions about driving at safe speeds." Allow time for student to share and fine-tune their sentences.

Examples

1. *Like Icarus, Bill ignored his father's instructions about driving at safe speeds.*
2. *Our football team's win over our cross-town rival was a Pyrrhic victory; we lost our starting quarterback, middle linebacker, and running back during the game to injury for the rest of the season.*
3. *A modern Antaeus, Mary always had a strong affinity for working in her garden.*
4. *The math quiz was a Gordian knot of impossible problems.*

55. GRADE A ALLUSIONS

Read the example paragraph on the handout about tofu. Ask students: "How do the allusions the writer uses reveal his attitude toward tofu?" Students should notice that the positive associations that go with the Holy Grail, Mecca, and Proteus work as metaphors that show the writer's admiration of tofu. Also point out that the model contains a specific claim and premise supported by both allusions and examples. Next, review with students what they will need to include in the paragraphs they write.

56. CELL PHONES

As you pass out this handout, read the example paragraph aloud. Ask students how the allusion to the Sirens relates to the writer's point and attitude. They should notice that the allusion works to enhance the writer's negative attitude toward cell phones. When students write their own paragraphs, you might broaden the topic to making a statement positively or negatively about any specific technology, such as computers, iPods, or electric pencil sharpeners.

57. ALLUSION MEETS ADVERTISING

Before giving students the handout, ask, "What would Pandora say if she were selling luggage?" If they recognize the allusion, they might make the connection between her box and luggage. Next, give students the handout and read the paragraph about Pandora. Point out that the writer in this passage takes on the persona, or voice, of Pandora by writing in the first person. As students write their own radio advertisements, remind them that they are taking on the voice of their people/characters. Set aside time for students to share their ads in class. For a follow-up activity, students might add music and/or sound effects and record the ads.

ALLUSION BACK STORIES

Achilles' heel: In the story from Greek mythology, Achilles' mother held him by the heels, dipping the infant in the river Styx in order to make him invulnerable. What she failed to realize, however, was that because her hand covered his heel area, Achilles was still vulnerable in that part of his body. Achilles was killed during the Trojan War when Paris shot an arrow at Achilles and pierced his heel. "Achilles' heel" refers to any individual's point of weakness or vulnerability.

Antaeus: A giant from Greek mythology who maintained his enormous strength as long as he remained in contact with the ground; his mother was Gaia, Mother Earth. Hercules met the undefeated Antaeus in a wrestling match and defeated him by holding him in the air and crushing him in a bear hug.

Big Brother: The dictatorial leader of the Totalitarian Party in George Orwell's novel *1984*. His portrait along with a caption reading, "Big Brother is watching!" is a reminder to the citizens of Oceania that they are constantly being monitored.

Catch-22: From the novel of the same name by Joseph Heller. The main character Yossarian is an American Air Force bombardier who attempts to avoid combat duty during World War II. He is presented with a dilemma called Catch-22: In order to be determined unfit for duty, he must be diagnosed as insane. However, this is impossible since anyone who wishes to avoid combat duty cannot be insane.

Cinderella: The fairy tale of a young woman who is taunted by her stepsisters and abused by her wicked stepmother. In the end, however, she wins by marrying the handsome prince.

Damascus Road: Traveling on the road to Damascus to persecute Christians who lived there, Saul was blinded by a light. He heard the voice of Jesus speaking to him. Based on this vision, he converted to Christianity, changed his name to Paul, and became one the great leaders of the early Christian church.

Don Quixote: A literary character created by Spanish author Miguel de Cervantes. An elderly man, Don Quixote is an avid reader of tales of chivalry and romance. Losing touch with reality one day, Don Quixote puts on rusty armor and jumps on his old horse to pursue adventure as a knight-errant.

Eden: The Garden of Paradise from the Old Testament book of Genesis. Eden was the home of Adam and Eve, the first man and woman, until they were cast out for their disobedience to God.

El Dorado: A mythical City of Gold that was said to exist somewhere in South America.

Gordian knot: In this legend, Alexander the Great takes on the challenge of untying an intricate knot. Knowing that it has been prophesized that whoever unties the knot will become king of Asia, Alexander slices the knot with a single sword stroke.

Hiroshima: The first city subjected to a nuclear bomb. More than 100,000 people died when the United States dropped an atomic bomb on this Japanese city on August 6, 1945.

Icarus: A character from Greek mythology. His father created a pair of wax wings for him and warned Icarus not to fly too close the sun. Icarus failed to heed his father's advice. When he flew too close to the sun, the wax melted, and Icarus fell into the sea.

Indiana Jones: The fictional adventurer and archeologist portrayed by Harrison Ford in several Hollywood films.

Judas: The disciple who betrayed Jesus to the Jewish authorities for thirty pieces of silver.

Luddites: Ned Ludd was the leader of a group of disgruntled 19th-century English textile workers. Upset that the new machinery of the Industrial Revolution was threatening their jobs, they destroyed the machines that they feared would replace them.

Midas: In Greek mythology, the god Dionysus granted King Midas one wish. Midas, greedy for riches, asked that everything that he touched would turn to gold. He soon regretted his request, when he touched his daughter and she turned to gold. He was also unable to eat because any food he touched turned into gold.

Pandora's box: In Greek mythology, Pandora was given a box by Zeus with instructions not to open it. Unable to overcome her curiosity, Pandora opened the box, releasing all the miseries and evil that afflicts humankind to this day.

Pontius Pilate: The Roman governor, who, in the New Testament gospels, presided over the trial of Jesus. He "washed his hands" of Jesus and released him to the Jewish authorities of Jerusalem.

Prometheus: A Titan from Greek mythology who defied the gods at Mount Olympus by stealing fire and giving it to humankind.

Pyrrhic victory: In victorious battles over the Roman Army in 280 B.C., King Pyrrhus of Epirus lost so many men that he was reported to utter, "One more such victory and we are undone." The Romans lost more men than Pyrrhus did in the battles, but because they had so many more soldiers than Pyrrhus, they were able to sustain their war effort. A Pyrrhic victory is one that comes at great cost.

Rubicon: In 49 B.C., Julius Caesar crossed the Rubicon River with his army in defiance of Roman law. Caesar's audacious act made armed conflict inevitable. As he crossed the river, legend reports that Caesar uttered the famous phrase, "The die is cast!"

Sisyphus: A king from Greek mythology who is punished by the gods for his transgressions in life. His task for eternity in Hades is to roll a huge stone to the top of a hill. After he rolls the stone to the summit of the hill, the stone then rolls down to the bottom of the hill, forcing Sisyphus to return and begin his task again.

Sour grapes: In a fable by Aesop, the fox attempts to reach some grapes high on a vine. Unable to get the grapes, he then rationalizes that the grapes were probably sour anyway.

The Tower of Babel: In a story from the Old Testament book of Genesis that takes place after the Great Flood, the citizens of Babel decide to build a great tower to the heavens. When God sees that the prideful people are working for their own glory and not for his, he confuses their languages and scatters them throughout the Earth.

Trojan horse: In its siege of Troy as told in Homer's *Iliad*, the Greeks built a huge wooden figure of a horse, with room enough inside to hide soldiers. After the Greeks pretended to sail away, the Trojans moved the horse into their walled city as a trophy. Late that night, the Greek soldiers crept out of the horse, opened the gates to the city to the rest of the Greek army, and proceeded to destroy the city of Troy. Since that time a "Trojan horse" has meant any trick or deception used to overcome an opponent.

Walter Mitty: The main character of a James Thurber short story. Mitty is an average man with a dull life who retreats to a life of adventure in his imaginative daydreams.

Watergate: Named for the Watergate Hotel in Washington, D.C., the 1970s Watergate political scandal began with a botched break-in that ultimately led to the resignation of President Richard Nixon and the indictment and conviction of several Nixon administration officials.

Syntax—Write Sentences That Are Clear, Varied, and Rhythmic

OVERVIEW

Mastery of the structure of sentences—syntax—is a hallmark of mature writing. Proficient writers craft sentences that are fluent, varied, and clear.

Chapters 9, 10, 11, and 12 will allow students to practice techniques that teach them how to write sentences using rhythm, balance, and repetition for effect. Students will learn to write effective, clear sentences that resonate in the reader's mind, memorable sentences that invite the reader to recite them out loud. Practicing the syntax activities in these chapters prepares them for integrating a variety of syntactical elements into the essays they will write in Part II.

Before introducing the activities in Chapters 9–12, do the following exercise as a whole-class activity.

PRE- AND POST-POINTS ACTIVITY: TACKLING SYNTAX

Before introducing students to the activities in Chapters 9–12, select one of the 101 topics from the list in "Resources." Write the question on the board, and create two columns that explore both sides of the question.

Example

Question: Is the pursuit of money a virtue or a vice? Explain.

Write a paragraph explaining three reasons you think the pursuit of money is a virtue.	Write a paragraph explaining three reasons you think the pursuit of money is a vice.

Tell students to pick one of the two sides of the question and to write a paragraph of at least five sentences arguing their case.

When students have finished, ask them to count the number of words in each of their sentences and write the numbers at the bottom of the paragraph. Explain to students that they will be exploring techniques to improve the sound, style, and structure of their sentences.

After completing Chapters 9–12, have students look back at the paragraphs they wrote during the pre-activity. Tell them to revise their sentences using what they have learned about parallelism, antithesis, alliteration, anaphora, and sentence length. The goal is to write sentences that are more varied, more interesting, and express thoughts more clearly. Once students have revised their paragraphs, have them write the number of words in each sentence. Then ask them to discuss the specific ways in which their revised paragraphs are better than their original versions.

If students are having trouble generating ideas for a paragraph, show them the following example.

Example

Write a paragraph explaining three reasons you think the pursuit of money is a vice.

Original

The pursuit of money is a vice. It blinds us to the important things in life. It causes us to work too hard. It causes us to waste time pursuing things rather than relationships. It has seductive charms. These charms make us forget the important things in life. Instead we follow money down a road to ruin. Following it makes our appetites insatiable. We want more and more. Our appetites are never satisfied.

Number of words in each sentence: 7, 9, 7, 11, 4, 10, 9, 6, 5, 5

Revised

Just grab a stick and poke your eye out. Like that stick, the pursuit of money is a vice that blinds us to the important things in life: our friends, family, and self worth. The money monster has an insatiable appetite that eats up our energy, our time, and our relationships. Money beckons us to the path to prosperity, but it leads us down the road of ruin. Stop where you are. Run in the opposite direction. Save your eyesight and your future.

Number of words in each sentence: 9, 25, 17, 17, 4, 5, 6

CHAPTER 9

Parallelism—Three-peat After Me

THE WHAT, WHY, AND HOW OF PARALLELISM

There is something special, perhaps even magical, about the number three. It's everywhere, it's omnipresent, and it's ubiquitous!

Speech coaches instruct their students to repeat a key idea three times so the audience will remember it. Advertisers create memorable slogans using three-beat lines: "The few, the proud, the Marines," or simple three-word slogans: "Just do it." Sales trainers teach salespeople to give the buyer three reasons to buy the product, three benefits of the product, three testimonials from satisfied customers, and finally, three choices on how to purchase the product.

In the world of rhetoric, however, the number three works its magic with two partners: rhythm and repetition. Together, they create a winning threesome— whether it be a sentence, statement, or rhetorical argument.

> *Lights! Camera! Action!*

> *I came, I saw, I conquered.* —Julius Caesar

> *The flocks fear the wolf, the crops the storm, and the trees the wind.* —Virgil

The human mind is built to patterns. Parallelism plugs the writer into the reader's innate desire for order and structure.

Parallelism is a big word for a simple concept: It is the repetition of the same word or syntactical structure. In the "Gettysburg Address," for example, Lincoln ends his speech by repeating the word *people* three times.

> *[T]his nation, under God, shall have a new birth of freedom—and that government of the people, by the people, for the people, shall not perish from the earth.*

But that's not all he repeats. Lincoln repeats the syntactical structure of three prepositional phrases, all with the word *people* as the object. This establishes a poetic, parallel rhythm that carries the sentence along and works to amplify the effect of the words.

Whether the writer is repeating words, phrases, or clauses, parallelism gives a sentence rhythm, balance, and clarity. It also makes a sentence more elaborate and more memorable. No wonder Lincoln used it as the clincher in his speech. He wanted to bring balance to a war-torn nation, and he wanted the idea of the restored unity of the United States to linger in the minds of his listeners as they left Gettysburg and returned to their homes.

The repetition of patterns and structures that a writer uses with parallelism gives the writing an intelligence and sophistication. When writers use parallelism, it is almost as if they are sending a subliminal message to the reader that says, "This writer is logical, lucid, and mature. Keep reading, keep reading, keep reading."

The activities in this chapter will introduce students to this secret weapon of style, showing them multiple examples and challenging them to apply parallelism in their own writing.

Chapter 9 Exercises

58. **Parallel Lines.** This activity clearly defines parallelism as students break down and analyze various examples.

59. **Parallelism in Action.** Students practice applying parallelism as they write original sentences.

60. **Tribute.** Students apply parallelism by writing about a person they admire.

61. **PSA.** Students use parallelism as they write an informative public-service announcement.

62. **Parallel Previews.** In this fun activity, students apply parallelism in an original movie preview.

58. PARALLEL LINES

Writing a sentence is like packing a suitcase: There is an art to getting everything in the bag—and not just getting it in, but keeping it all organized and accessible. Parallelism is the secret weapon for writers who pack sentences, not suitcases: It helps them (and you) to pack a lot of ideas into a sentence in an orderly, logical way.

Parallelism is a big word for a simple concept: It means that you repeat the same structure in a sentence. Notice, for example, how the following words from John F. Kennedy's inaugural address are coherently packed into a single sentence by using parallel verb phrases.

> Let every nation know, whether it wishes us well or ill, that we shall pay any price, bear any burden, meet any hardship, support any friend, oppose any foe, in order to assure the survival and the success of liberty.

Notice that parallelism is not just the repetition of the same words—it is the repetition of the same structure. Whether the writer is repeating words, phrases, or clauses, parallelism gives a sentence rhythm, balance, and clarity.

Directions

Re-write the following quotations, arranging the words so that the parallel words, phrases, or clauses are below each other.

Example
Original

> There are no secrets to success. It is the result of preparation, hard work, and learning from failure. —Colin L. Powell

Revised

> There are no secrets to success. It is the result of
> preparation,
> hard work, and
> learning from failure. —Colin L. Powell

1. *I have fought the good fight, I have finished my course, I have kept the faith.* —2 Timothy 4:7
2. *I am seeking, I am striving, I am in it with all my heart.* —Vincent van Gogh
3. *Life is a compromise of what your ego wants to do, what experience tells you to do, and what your nerves let you do.* —Bruce Crampton
4. *In company with our brave Allies and brothers-in-arms on other Fronts you will bring about the destruction of the German war machine, the elimination of Nazi tyranny over oppressed peoples of Europe, and security for ourselves in a free world.* —Dwight D. Eisenhower
5. *The only thing we have to fear is fear itself—nameless, unreasoning, unjustified terror which paralyzes needed efforts to convert retreat into advance.* —Franklin Delano Roosevelt

59. PARALLELISM IN ACTION

The rhythm, balance, and clarity of parallelism make it a great strategy for capturing your reader's attention right from the start. Notice how the writers in the following three examples use parallelism in the first sentences of their short stories.

Examples

I'm tired of this weather. It's so unpredictable. In the past few days I played soccer in the snow, ate ice cream in a thunderstorm, and went snowboarding in a heat wave. How am I supposed to enjoy my summer this way?

"And after you're done, pick up my dry cleaning," said Melinda, and with a slam of a door, she was gone. "Yes, queen of all that is bratty," mumbled Cindy, scrubbing the floor. "Oh, that lady is crazy," thought Cindy. "All I do every day is dry clean her clothes, dry clean her cat, and dry clean her wigs."

The rural street lies desolate, save for a few crows pecking at food scraps on the road. The front door to a run-down home opens, and out steps a man, visibly shaken as he walks to his car. He wipes several beads of sweat off his forehead, grips his concealed pistol, and opens the car door.

Directions

Write an opening to a short story with at least one sentence using parallelism. To add additional dramatic tension, put your characters in some kind of specific conflict right from the start, and include some dialogue.

_____

_____

_____

_____

_____

_____

_____

_____

_____

_____

60. TRIBUTE

Old myths, old gods, old heroes have never died. They are only sleeping at the bottom of our mind, waiting for our call. We have need for them. They represent the wisdom of our race. —Stanley Kunitz

Directions

What one person has made a significant difference in making the world a better place? What specifically has he or she done? Write about someone famous or someone you know personally. Use parallelism in some of your sentences.

Example

He was named the man of the millennium by Life magazine; he was Parade Magazine's top American innovator; and in a book that ranked the most influential persons of all time, he made it into the top 40. He died in 1931, but no one has come close to the creative energy, productivity, and positive attitude of Thomas Edison. Holder of over 1,000 patents, his inventions touched and changed the lives of every man, woman, and child in America. The light bulb, phonograph, motion-picture camera, telegraph, telephone, and typewriter are just a few of the devices he either developed or improved. It's no wonder he created so much, since he was a tireless worker: sometimes he would spend up to one hundred nights in a row working in his lab without returning home. Although he had only four months of formal education and although one of his teachers labeled him "retarded," he pursued his own education, and he achieved so much that today his name is synonymous with genius. In Edison, the three chords of imagination, perspiration, and innovation combined to create a symphony of achievements that remind us that the only limits that exist in this world are the limits we create in our own minds.

61. PSA

Directions

Write the text of a radio public-service announcement (PSA) on any issue concerning safety, health, education, law, or finance. Use humor to keep the audiences' attention. Use some sentences with parallelism to pack plenty of details into your announcement.

Use one of the following topics or come up with your own.

Dangers of:

drinking too much coffee

too much Internet surfing

too much fast food

falling asleep in class

too much karaoke

Benefits of:

maintaining a positive relationship with your teacher or parents

unicycle riding

good attendance at school

playing a sport

reading works by your favorite author

Example

Three colorful spheres fly through the air in a mesmerizing pattern. This three-ball cascade is not being performed by some juggling jester or circus clown. Instead, this gravity-defying feat is being done by Mary Johnson, a 35-year-old mother of three who juggles alone in her living room every afternoon. Mary isn't looking for an audience to entertain. She's looking to keep her mind young and agile and sharp. Everyone should try juggling, not only because it's fun, but also because it builds the brain. German researchers completed a study that showed adults who practiced juggling for a period of three months showed increased gray matter; in contrast, adults who did not juggle in the study showed no increase in brain size. Many people associate juggling with clowns, but with practice and persistence anyone can learn to juggle and reap its mental benefits. In addition to the brain boost documented by German researchers, it's also great exercise, a great way to learn to focus on the matter at hand, and a great way to improve hand-eye coordination. A larger brain, a smaller waistline, an increased ability to focus, and decreased worry about losing your mind—no wonder Mary Johnson juggles even when no one is watching.

62. PARALLEL PREVIEWS

Directions

Write the text of a voice-over for a new movie trailer for your favorite movie or write about an imaginary movie of your own creation. Use parallelism to add some rhythm and resonance to your preview. The following example is the movie trailer for *Hamlet, Prince of Denmark*.

> *Mourning his dead father, berating his clueless mother, and continually contemplating the murder of his remorseless, treacherous, and lecherous uncle, Hamlet is not having a good day! Something, indeed, is rotten in the state of Denmark, and it's not just the fish from last week's dinner that has been festering in the corner of the Castle Elsinore's kitchen.*

Chapter 9 Teaching Notes and Answers

58. PARALLEL LINES

Give students the handout, and read the opening simile that compares parallelism to packing a suitcase. The point here is that parallelism helps writers make sure their ideas are clear, orderly, and easy to find.

Parallelism also makes a sentence more elaborate and more memorable. Consider showing students the following passage, in which William Golding, in his novel *Lord of the Flies*, uses parallel verb phrases in two successive sentences to describe his young protagonist, Ralph.

> *Then he leapt back on the terrace, pulled off his shirt, and stood there among the skull-like coconuts with green shadows from the palms and the forest sliding over his skin. He undid the snake-clasp of his belt, lugged off his shorts and pants, and stood there naked, looking at the dazzling beach and the water.*

The following are some additional sentences you can use as models.

1. *To get profit without risk, experience without danger and reward without work is as impossible as it is to live without being born.* —A.P. Gouthey
2. *The great rock loitered, poised on one toe, decided not to return, moved through the air, fell, struck, turned over, leapt droning through the air and smashed a deep hole in the canopy of the forest.* —William Golding
3. *Hannah prepares her special energy drink by placing a one-pound block of Spam into the blender, pouring in a half-gallon of buttermilk, and mixing on medium for three minutes.*
4. *Max loves writing sonorous sentences that startle the stubborn, crafting crackling clauses that confound the cautious, and forging fantastic phrases that frighten the fainthearted.*
5. *His textbooks under his arm, his eyes focused straight ahead, and his mind preoccupied with his upcoming math test, Sam walked briskly through the cafeteria.*

Answers

1. *I have fought the good fight,*
   I have finished my course,
   I have kept the faith.
2. *I am seeking,*
   I am striving,
   I am in it with all my heart.
3. *Life is a compromise of*
   what your ego wants to do,
   what experience tells you to do, and
   what your nerves let you do.

4. *In company with our brave Allies and brothers-in-arms on other Fronts you will bring about*
   the destruction of the German war machine,
   the elimination of Nazi tyranny over oppressed peoples of Europe, and
   security for ourselves in a free world.
5. *The only thing we have to fear is fear itself—*
   nameless,
   unreasoning,
   unjustified terror, which paralyzes needed efforts to convert retreat into advance.

59. PARALLELISM IN ACTION

After passing out the handout, read the three examples with students. Ask them to underline the parallel parts of each passage as you read them. Briefly go over each quote to show the elements that are parallel. Then ask students to complete the assignment by writing their own opening to a short story. Make sure to set aside time later for students to share their openings to see how well they hook an audience.

60. TRIBUTE

Read through the example paragraph about Edison. As students read, ask them to underline examples of parallelism and think about how the writer's use of parallelism adds to the passage. They should notice that parallelism adds rhythm and allows the writer to elaborate on the achievements and positive attributes of Edison. Students should brainstorm to choose their famous people and not necessarily write about their immediate, first choices. Provide some time for research before students begin their drafts, if needed.

61. PSA

Before giving students the handout, ask them if they have heard any memorable PSAs. Ask them how using parallelism in an informative announcement like a PSA might contribute to how well the audience remembers its message. Students should recognize that parallelism would add the kind of rhythm, balance, and clarity that makes a message memorable. Pass out the handout, and read the PSA about juggling with students as they highlight examples of parallelism. As students prepare to write their own PSAs, point out the ideas listed on the handout, but also call on students to offer additional ideas of interest.

62. PARALLEL PREVIEWS

Have students read the example movie trailer about *Hamlet* before writing their own trailers. Ask them to highlight the examples of parallelism and to make sure that they include parallelism in their own pieces. Allow some time for students to share their trailers.

CHAPTER **10**

Antithesis—Opposites Attract

KEY TERMS

Antithesis: The juxtaposition of contrasting ideas in parallel words, phrases, or clauses, such as: *To err is human, to forgive divine.*

THE WHAT, WHY, AND HOW OF ANTITHESIS

Outside of a dog, a book is man's best friend.
Inside of a dog it's too dark to read anyway. —Groucho Marx

Live as if you were to die tomorrow.
Learn as if you were to live forever. —Mahatma Gandhi

To err is human, to forgive divine. —Alexander Pope

What do the three quotes above have in common with the first words spoken from the surface of the moon?

On July 20, 1969, Neil A. Armstrong became the first man on the moon. As he took his first step off the lunar module, he immediately uttered a verbal misstep. Instead of saying "That's one small step for 'a' man; one giant leap for mankind," he left out the word "a," saying "That's one small step for man; one giant leap for mankind."

Instead of criticizing Armstrong's flub, we should honor his effort in crafting a memorable sentence that was structured to capture the magnitude of the moment. In punctuating mankind's most remarkable technological achievement, Armstrong used *antithesis*, a structured form that dates back to the classical orators of ancient Greece and Rome. As a word, antithesis means "the exact opposite," as in *love* is the opposite of *hate*. But as a figure of speech, antithesis juxtaposes contrasting ideas in a balanced manner, or—as in Armstrong's case—a contrast of degrees: *small step* versus *giant leap* and *man* versus *mankind*.

We live in a world of dichotomies: *hot/cold, light/dark, tragedy/comedy, love/hate.* Antithesis is the technique of juxtaposing these opposites. Notice, for example, how the sentences that open this chapter play with contrasts and parallelism to make concise, clear, and balanced statements.

Using antithesis creates contrast but also brings a balance, revealing the tone of someone who sees the world in all of its broad contrasts and particular opposites. When writers use antithesis, the contrasts and opposition create a tension that keep the reader interested. When ideas clash, something is at stake, so there's more reason for the reader to stick around; a reader might even forget that he's reading an essay and pay attention to the fact that a real person with a real voice stands behind the words. The presence of opposites also enhances the writer's stature, making the reader more confident that the writer is a person who sees the big picture and is not limited to one side of an issue.

Antithesis creates balance through opposition. It also takes advantage of the reader's innate interest in conflict. The activities in this chapter will show students antithesis in action in a variety of different ways, and they provide an opportunity to practice this powerful technique.

Chapter 10 Exercises

63. **Spot the Antithesis.** This activity shows students a variety of examples that use antithesis.

64. **Proverbial Antithesis.** This activity illustrates the powerful punch of antithesis in concise, yet memorable, proverbs.

65. **Balanced Antithesis.** Students practice revising sentences using antithesis.

66. **Claiming a Contrast.** Students apply antithesis to write about contrasting ideas.

67. **Focused Contrast.** Students include antithesis as they write a comparison composition about a person, place, or thing of their choice.

68. **Four-word Dramatic Dialogue.** Students apply antithesis as they write a brief dialogue.

63. SPOT THE ANTITHESIS

Notice how the following well-known sayings use antithesis and parallelism for a pleasing, balanced effect. They didn't become proverbial sayings by accident. Instead, they were carefully crafted by someone who understood that opposites attract.

> *Give him an inch, and he'll take a mile.*

> *If we don't hang together, we will hang separately.*

> *United we stand, divided we fall.*

Contrast is one key to clear prose. You can make a word or idea clear by telling what it is, but you can make a word or idea even clearer by telling what it is not. When you give a friend driving directions to your home, for example, you can tell her which way to go to get there, but really good directions also give the driver pitfalls to avoid and landmarks to look for if she gets lost.

Directions

Read the following quotes and write down the two opposing ideas that make up the antithesis.

1. _____/_____ *There is work that is work and there is play that is play; there is play that is work and work that is play. And in only one of these lies happiness.* —Gelett Burgess

2. _____/_____ *To every disadvantage there is a corresponding advantage.* —W. Clement Stone

3. _____/_____ *Today the real test of power is not capacity to make war but capacity to prevent it.* —Anne O'Hare McCormick

4. _____/_____ *Now is the winter of our discontent /Made glorious summer by this son of York.* —William Shakespeare

5. _____/_____ *Some men see things as they are and say, "Why?" I dream things that never were and say, "Why not?"* —Robert F. Kennedy

6. _____/_____ *In the depth of winter, I finally learned that there was in me an invincible summer.* —Albert Camus

7. _____/_____ *The world will little note, nor long remember, what we say here, but it can never forget what they did here.* —Abraham Lincoln

64. PROVERBIAL ANTITHESIS

Directions

Antithesis packs the kind of punch that makes it memorable. See if you can complete the following familiar proverbs by inserting the antithetical elements. Don't worry about coming up with the right answer. Instead, just try for a pair of opposites that might work.

Examples

_____ is stranger than _____.
Truth/fiction or *Captain Kirk/Spock*

One man's _____ is another man's _____.
Meat/poison or *music/noise*

1. _____ speaks louder than _____.

2. The best _____ is a good _____.

3. If you want _____, prepare for _____.

4. If you are not a part of the _____, you are a part of the _____.

5. _____ and the world laughs with you; _____ and you weep alone.

6. A _____ is not believed when he tells the _____.

7. Never put off until _____ what you can do _____.

8. One is _____ until proven _____.

9. One must _____ before he _____.

10. One _____ is worth a thousand _____.

65. BALANCED ANTITHESIS

A little antithesis can go a long way in its power to transform a sentence from average to amazing.

Example

Original: *We were laughing at the beginning of the movie, but at the end of the movie we all began to cry.*

Revised: *We were laughing at the beginning of the movie. We were crying at the end.*

Directions

Revise the following sentences using antithesis to make the sentences balanced and parallel.

1. *Our coach talked to us about learning from defeat. Learning from victory was what our team captain always talked about.*

   _____

   _____

2. *The Johnson family travels to the lake each summer. Each winter, they travel to the ski lodge.*

   _____

   _____

3. *Success requires hard work and sacrifice. Little is required to fail.*

   _____

   _____

4. *Mary's teacher was always talking about logic, but creativity was what Mary was thinking about.*

   _____

   _____

5. *In the morning we were excited to get to work, but we were anxious to get home by nightfall.*

   _____

   _____

66. CLAIMING A CONTRAST

IDEAS FOR ANTITHESIS

above/below	hot/cold	quantity/quality
abstract/concrete	inside/outside	quickly/slowly
actions/words	intelligence/stupidity	read/write
always/never	joy/sorrow	rich/poor
attack/defend	laugh/cry	run/walk
before/after	left/right	save/spend
beginning/end	literal/figurative	speak/listen
celebrate/mourn	logic/creativity	study/cram
confidence/self doubt	loss/gain	success/failure
dark/light	male/female	tragedy/comedy
early/late	nature/nurture	truth/falsehood
fact/opinion	order/chaos	urban/rural
fast/slow	parent/child	victory/defeat
freedom/slavery	power/impotence	war/peace
friend/enemy	present/past	words/pictures
good/evil	prudence/rashness	yesterday/today

Directions

Select a topic and write an opening sentence that makes a claim based on the differences in the two topics, such as:

Logic teaches us about the world; creativity teaches us about ourselves.

Then write a short composition of at least 150 words in which you support the claim using contrast, details, examples, evidence, and a full-circle conclusion.

Example

When we read, we travel to a world of imagination; when we write, we imagine a world of our own. With reading, the words are fixed on the page for us, and although words evoke different pictures in the minds of different readers, we still are limited by the words the author selected for us. When Robert Frost, for example, describes the snow, he says, "The only other sound's the sweep of easy wind and downy flake." Whoever reads this imagines falling snow. When we write, however, we are in control of the words we choose and, therefore, the worlds—and the weather—we create. We become omniscient and omnipotent. If we choose, we can defy gravity, we can defy logic, we can defy nature. If we choose we can create a snowstorm in August, a world where words grow on trees, where trees speak in Latin. Reading exercises our imagination, opening our eyes to see more; writing challenges our imagination, forcing our minds to be more.

67. FOCUSED CONTRAST

Directions

Argue that one person, place, thing, or idea is superior to another person, place, thing, or idea. To focus your comparison and contrast, make sure you identify the specific area of comparison in your premise.

Example

> Reagan was a better president than Eisenhower <u>because of his superior vision for America.</u>

> Dogs are better pets than cats <u>because they provide more services for their owners.</u>

Then, write a short composition where you support your claim and premise with evidence, examples, and details. Because you are using contrast, include at least one sentence with antithesis somewhere in your paragraph.

> Someone once said, "Dogs have owners; cats have staff." Dogs are better pets than cats because of the fact that they provide more services for their owners. Throughout history, dogs have bonded with humans by working with and for them to complete important tasks, such as hunting, herding, and guarding. Sure, cats may catch mice, but they do this out of instinct, not out of love for their owners. The bark of a dog is an alarm that sounds a warning that a stranger is approaching. Ask any burglar; they will tell you that the bark of an alert, watchful dog is a sure-fire deterrent to any thief. In addition to guarding the house, dogs also get their owners out of the house for valuable exercise. Some might see this as a negative, but the truth is a good, brisk walk is as valuable and therapeutic for the owner as it is for the dog. Last, but possibly most important, is the emotional bond between a dog and its owner. Where else can a person find the kind of unconditional love offered by Fido? He is faithful, unselfish, and true. Whether his master is a prince or a pauper, prosperous or poor, healthy or sick, the dog stands by his master's side. When all others desert the owner, the dog remains, alert and ready to serve.

68. FOUR-WORD DRAMATIC DIALOGUE

Directions

Write a dramatic scene between two characters involved in some kind of conflict. The catch is that every line of dialogue must be exactly four words—no more, no less! You may pick familiar characters from literature, television, history, film, or even current events. Or you may use generic characters, such as father/son, teacher/student, boss/worker, girl/boy, etc. Include a four-word title.

Example

Star Wars Episode XXIV

Darth Vader:	*Luke, I'm your father!*
Luke:	*Where have you been?*
Darth Vader:	*Busy working long hours.*
Luke:	*Couldn't you have written?*
Darth Vader:	*Sorry. Really, I'm sorry!*
Luke:	*The Dark Side sucks!*
Darth Vader:	*Here are some gifts.*
Luke:	*Thanks a lot, Father.*
Darth Vader:	*They're not from me.*
Luke:	*Who are they from?*
Darth Vader:	*They are from Yoda.*
Luke:	*They're wrapped very nicely.*
Darth Vader:	*They are great gifts!*
Luke:	*How do you know?*
Darth Vader:	*I felt your presents.*

Chapter 10 Teaching Notes and Answers

63. SPOT THE ANTITHESIS

Before you pass out this handout, write one of the proverbial sayings from the handout on the board, such as "United we stand; divided we fall." Ask students why a concise statement like this is memorable. Students may not have heard of antithesis, but they may notice the way the quote uses contrasts like united/divided and stand/fall to create an interesting contrast.

Next, pass out the handout and read through the explanation and examples of antithesis. Go through the problems together, so that students get a feel for the different ways writers use antithesis in the problems. The following are some additional examples.

1. *Happiness is <u>good</u> health and a <u>bad</u> memory.* —Ingrid Bergman
2. *Those who <u>cast</u> the votes decide <u>nothing</u>. Those who <u>count</u> the votes decide <u>everything</u>.* —Joseph Stalin
3. *It is more blessed to <u>give</u> than to <u>receive</u>.* —Acts 20:35

Answers
1. Work/play
2. Disadvantage/advantage
3. Make war/prevent war
4. Winter/summer
5. Things that are; why/things that never were; why not
6. Winter/summer
7. Remember; say/ forget; did

64. PROVERBIAL ANTITHESIS

As students proceed through this activity, accept any answer, as long as the two ideas contrast. Students may not be familiar with proverbial sayings such as "Actions speak louder than words," so be prepared for creative answers. The key here is to illustrate that antithesis is an excellent tool for creating concise, clear, and interesting statements.

Possible Answers
1. actions/words
2. defense/offense
3. peace/war
4. solution/problem
5. laugh/weep
6. liar/truth
7. today/tomorrow
8. innocent/guilty
9. crawl/walks
10. picture/words

65. BALANCED ANTITHESIS

Before passing out the handout, read through the example original sentence along with the revision that uses antithesis. Point out that the revision provides more parallel, balanced, and interesting writing.

Possible Answers

1. *Our coach talked to us about learning from defeat; our team captain talked to us about learning from victory.*
2. *The Johnson family travels to the lake each summer; they travel to the ski lodge each winter.*
3. *Success requires hard work and sacrifice; failure requires little.*
4. *Mary's teacher was always talking about logic, but Mary was always thinking about creativity.*
5. *In the morning we were excited to get to work, but by nightfall, we were anxious to get home.*

66. CLAIMING A CONTRAST

As you pass out this handout, have students look at the "Ideas for Antithesis," and note the great variety of contrast available to any writer. Next, read the example passage on the handout. As you read, have student highlight examples of antithesis in the passage. Ask them how the writer's use of antithesis enhances the passage. They should notice how the contrast of reading with writing helps the reader to see both topics in a better light.

67. FOCUSED CONTRAST

After passing out the handout, read the sample passage, "Every Day is a Dog Day." Ask students to highlight the area of comparison on which the writer focuses, and ask them also to identify examples of antithesis. Encourage students to brainstorm some ideas for their own contrast, and challenge them to go beyond the first idea that pops into their minds. Consider giving students some time to brainstorm ideas in small groups before they begin writing their pieces.

68. FOUR-WORD DRAMATIC DIALOGUE

As you pass out this handout, ask for two volunteers to read the example dialogue between Darth Vader and Luke. Next, ask students to brainstorm other possible characters they might write about. Since this is a dialogue, working in pairs makes sense. Emphasize that each line of dialogue must be exactly four words, and that the dialogue will be more interesting if the characters are in some kind of conflict. Schedule some time for students to read, and possibly even perform, their dialogues at a later date.

Alliteration and Anaphora— You Can Say That Again

KEY TERMS

Alliteration: The repetition of initial sounds of words. For example, *You are either green and growing or ripe and rotting.*

Anaphora: The repetition of the initial words in phrases, clauses, or sentences, such as the following quotation from Winston Churchill: *We shall fight on the beaches, we shall fight on the landing grounds, we shall fight in the streets, we shall fight in the hills, we shall never surrender.*

Assonance: The repetition of internal vowels, as in *fit as a fiddle.*

Consonance: The repetition of internal consonants, *as in o**dd**s and en**ds**, and la**st** but not lea**st**.*

THE WHAT, WHY, AND HOW OF ALLITERATION AND ANAPHORA

> *The one animal that has been domesticated by man without discarding its dignity, the one animal that is loyal to its master without losing its independence, the one animal that will serve without being a slave is the cat. He will faithfully show up to be fed every day but refuse to follow a schedule. He will approach you with elegance and grace, allowing you to stroke his soft fur, but he will refuse to bend to base commands. No saying "sit" to him, no fetching flung objects. Drooling on davenports is beneath his dignity. Being led on a leash is ludicrous. Once deified by the Egyptians, the cat has not forgotten his regal roots, his imperial heritage. He will kill a mouse for you, but he will never allow you to kill his spirit.*

The passage above uses more than just logic and facts to make a case for owning a cat. It employs two powerful rhetorical devices called *alliteration* and *anaphora*.

Alliteration, the repetition of the initial sounds in words, gives portions of the above passage an echoing emphasis that resonates in the mind and the ears of the reader. *Anaphora*, the purposeful repetition of words at the beginning of phrases, clauses, or sentences, gives the passage a rhythmic, lyrical quality.

Prominent writers and orators know the power of properly placed, repeated words and sounds. They know the power of reason, but they also know the power of resonance. Readers read with both their eyes and their ears, looking for both sound and sense.

Good writers know they need to arrange their words so they explain, but they also need to arrange their words so they echo. The activities in this chapter will show students how two small rhetorical touches can add a lot of life to their writing.

See "Teaching Notes and Answers" at the end of this chapter for additional examples of alliteration and anaphora.

Chapter 11 Exercises

69. **Repetition for a Reason.** This activity will help student see the prevalence of anaphora and alliteration in everyday language, especially in everyday memorable language.

70. **Echoing Words and Sounds.** Students practice distinguishing between alliteration and anaphora and understand how using them can add eloquence and energy to a sentence.

71. **Reruns Worth Watching: Alliteration and Anaphora.** Students see a variety of examples of alliteration and anaphora in action.

72. **One Change.** Students apply alliteration and anaphora while writing about their own original ideas.

73. **Overrated/Underrated.** Students apply alliterations and anaphora as they write to a topic they are passionate about.

74. **Composition Replete with Repetitive T's:** Students practice writing with repeated words and sounds in this fun activity.

75. **Alliterative Antithesis Hook and Full-circle Conclusion.** Students practice applying alliteration and anaphora to the hook and ending of a short essay.

69. REPETITION FOR A REASON

In the English language, the sound of a sentence can reinforce the sense of a sentence. Many of our familiar popular sayings, expressions, and buzzwords feature alliteration and anaphora. This is not coincidence. Instead, it is because alliteration and anaphora make the language memorable through the repetition and the resonance of words and sounds. With literally thousands of words at our disposal, our mother tongue is a language abounding in a treasure trove of sonorous syllables. Here are some examples.

Anaphora
day in, day out
put up or shut up
first come, first served
don't call us, we'll call you
united we stand, divided we fall
thanks, but no thanks

Alliteration
gas guzzler
tried and true
mind over matter
sink or swim
calm, cool, and collected
left in the lurch

Directions

See if you can identify the repeated words that are used to create anaphora in the following familiar sayings.

1. *March comes in _____ a lion and goes out _____ a lamb.*

2. *The _____ things change, the _____ they stay the same.*

3. *_____ see, _____ do.*

4. *No _____ is good _____.*

5. *_____ pain, _____ gain.*

6. *_____ ventured, _____ gained.*

7. *A _____ saved is a _____ earned.*

8. *One _____ trash is another _____ treasure.*

9. *The only thing we have to _____ is _____ itself.*

10. *_____ _____, and absolute _____ _____ absolutely.*

Now try to identify the missing words in the following familiar sayings that feature alliteration.

1. *A m_____ is as good as a m_____.*

2. *Parting is s_____ s_____ s_____.*

3. *P_____ what you p_____.*

4. *The p_____ is in the p_____.*

5. *S_____ the rod, s_____ the child.*

6. *Don't throw the b_____ out with the b_____ water.*

7. *The spirit is w_____ but the flesh is w_____.*

8. *S_____ and s_____ wins the race.*

9. *T_____ and t_____ wait for no man.*

10. *L_____, l_____, and the pursuit of happiness.*

70. ECHOING WORDS AND SOUNDS

Read the following two passages. In the first, Annie Dillard talks about a brief encounter with a moth. In the second, Steven Johnson talks about modern youth.

> *A golden female moth, a biggish one with a two-inch wingspan, flapped into the fire, dropped her abdomen into the wet wax, stuck, flamed, frazzled, and fried in a second.*

> *Today's kids see the screen as an environment to be explored, inhabited, shared, and shaped. They're blogging. They're building their MySpace pages. They're constructing elaborate fan sites for their favorite artists and TV shows. They're playing immensely complicated games, such as Civilization IV—one of the most popular computer games in the U.S. last fall—in which players re-create the entire course of human economic and technological history.*

In the first passage, Dillard uses *alliteration*, the repetition of the initial sounds in words, for emphasis that resonates in the mind and the ears of the reader. In the second passage, Johnson uses *anaphora*, the purposeful repetition of words at the beginning of phrases, clauses, or sentences, to give the passage a rhythmic, lyrical quality.

Alliteration and anaphora are rhetorical reruns that repeat sound and words for effect and for emphasis. In moderation, alliteration accentuates the sense of a sentence via repeated sounds within the sentence. With anaphora, the right word repeated at the right time and the right place in your writing will give it eloquence, emphasis, and energy.

Directions

Read the following passage. As you read, mark any instances of alliteration or anaphora. How many of each can you find?

> *The one animal that has been domesticated by man without discarding its dignity, the one animal that is loyal to its master without losing its independence, the one animal that will serve without being a slave is the cat. He will faithfully show up to be fed every day but refuse to follow a schedule. He will approach you with elegance and grace, allowing you to stroke his soft fur, but he will refuse to bend to base commands. No saying "sit" to him, no fetching flung objects. Drooling on davenports is beneath his dignity. Being led on a leash is ludicrous. Once deified by the Egyptians, the cat has not forgotten his regal roots, his imperial heritage. He will kill a mouse for you, but he will never allow you to kill his spirit.*

Number of instances of alliteration: _____

Number of instances of anaphora: _____

71. RERUNS WORTH WATCHING: ALLITERATION AND ANAPHORA

In moderation, alliteration packs the proper punch to punctuate a point. Be careful, though: like too much cologne, too much make-up, or the previous sentence, alliteration can call attention to itself and distract the reader from the sense behind the sound.

In addition to the repetition of initial sounds, writers can also capitalize on the repetition of sounds inside of words. The repetition of internal vowels is called *assonance* while the repetition of internal consonants is called *consonance*. Notice, for example, how Mark Twain repeats the /O/ and /L/ sounds in the following description of the Mississippi River:

> *A broad expanse of the river was turned to blood; in the middle distance the red hue brightened into gold, through which a solitary log came floating, black and conspicuous; in one place a long, slanting mark lay sparkling upon the water; in another the surface was broken by boiling, tumbling rings that were as many-tinted as an opal.*

Anaphora is "parallelism plus." Whereas parallelism (Chapter 9) is the repetition of grammatical structures, anaphora adds repetition of the same word or words at the beginning of a phrase, a clause, or a sentence.

Normally, repetition in writing is something to be avoided, but applied at the right time, for effect, repetition creates an emphasis and an eloquence that gives an ordinary passage a powerful resonance.

Directions

Read the following quotations and identify each as using either alliteration or anaphora. Remember, alliteration is the repetition of sound, and anaphora is the repetition of words.

1. *An aphorism is the last link in a long chain of thought.* —Marie Von Ebner-Eschenbach
2. *Never give in—never, never, never, in nothing great or small, large or petty, never give in except to convictions of honor and good sense.* —Winston Churchill
3. *Beware the barrenness of a busy life.* —Socrates
4. *But, in a larger sense, we cannot dedicate—we cannot consecrate—we cannot hallow—this ground. The brave men, living and dead, who struggled here, have consecrated it, far above our poor power to add or detract.* —Abraham Lincoln
5. *To convince is to conquer without conception.* —Walter Benjamin
6. *We can learn much from wise words, little from wisecracks, and less from wise guys.* —William Arthur Ward
7. *A definition is the enclosing of a wilderness of idea within a wall of words.* —Samuel Butler

72. ONE CHANGE

Every great dream begins with a dreamer. Always remember, you have within you the strength, the patience, and the passion to reach for the stars to change the world. —Harriet Tubman

Directions

If you had the power, what one change would you make to improve your town, your country, or your world? Identify the change you would make, why it is necessary, and specifically how it would be an improvement. Write at least 200 words using alliteration and/or anaphora to punctuate key points of your argument.

Example

A child sits mesmerized by the magical movie The Wizard of Oz. *She's immersed in a wonderful story and the imaginative world of Dorothy. Unfortunately, she is watching the film on cable television, so just as she becomes engrossed in this world of wonder, she is jolted back to the harsh reality of a world that wants to sell her shampoo, breakfast cereal, and cold medicine. The worst thing on television is the commercials because they interrupt the viewer's train of thought, discouraging concentration. And these commercial interruptions don't just happen once or twice, they happen at least every fifteen minutes. No wonder even adults have a hard time focusing on anything for more than a few minutes; television's commercialism is designed to discourage concentration, discourage cognition, and discourage communication. Instead of enjoying a coherent narrative over the course of a one- or two-hour period, television shocks and jolts its viewers with a nonsensical array of incoherent messages and images. In a modern age that is already deluged with distractions, who needs to submit themselves to more? Instead, turn off the TV and pick up a book so that you can enjoy a good story at your own pace. And if you do watch* The Wizard of Oz, *at least get the DVD so you can watch it without interruptions.*

73. OVERRATED/UNDERRATED

Directions

What is something you think is either overrated or underrated? Construct an argument of at least 150 words with a claim, at least three premises, evidence, and explanation. Use alliteration and/or anaphora to highlight your adulation or your abhorrence of your selected topic.

Example

Walking is underrated. It benefits the body, the mind, and the pocketbook. If everyone in the U.S. were to walk briskly for just thirty minutes per day, we would cut the incidences of chronic diseases dramatically. Walking reduces the risk of heart disease, the risk of diabetes, the risk of arthritis, and the risk of cancer. It's also good for the mind since studies show that walking reduces the likelihood of clinical depression. Smart seniors know the psychological value of staying active, breathing fresh air, and saving their hard-earned dollars by paying less for gas. Instead of venerating our motor vehicle-obsessed society, we should celebrate citizens who stroll along the sidewalks of suburbia. More walkers mean less traffic, less pollution, and less wasted gas money. With so many potential positives, no one should view walking as a pain anymore.

_____

_____

_____

_____

_____

_____

_____

_____

_____

_____

_____

_____

_____

_____

74. COMPOSITION REPLETE WITH REPETITIVE T'S

Directions

Stipulating that writing must contain the letter "t," the most frequently utilized consonant, the teacher momentarily lost touch with sanity. The teacher then continued to task students to write different writing types containing the letter "t." The teacher told the students, "Utilize this list."

Composition Types to Try

advertisements	*metaphors*
alliterative poetry	*mysteries*
arguments	*reports*
autobiographic anecdotes	*short stories*
descriptions	*skits*
detective stories	*sonnets*
diatribes	*tall tales*
editorials	*television sitcom scripts*
interviews	*tragedies*
letters	*tongue-twisters*

Criteria: Creativity, clarity, jocularity, lucidity, timeliness, technique, narrative originality, character development, editing, sentence structure, grammatical correctness.

Caveat: Writing compositions replete with the letter "t" might turn tragic. Students often get addicted. They can't stop writing with T's. Therefore, try to contain writing to ten compositions tops! Thanks.

In case you didn't notice, every word in the above directions contains at least one "t." Try emulating this insanity! Write a passage of at least 100 words on a topic of your choice using at least one "t" in each word. Try mixing in some anaphora and alliteration for good measure.

75. ALLITERATIVE ANTITHESIS HOOK AND FULL-CIRCLE CONCLUSION

You can use alliteration and antithesis to hook your reader's interest or to end your essay.

An alliterative antithesis hook. Antithesis helps a writer achieve both balance and contrast; alliteration helps a writer achieve both resonance and rhythm. Antithesis makes a strong first impression on your reader by beginning with a balanced sentence that features contrasting, clashing ideas. In addition, adding some alliteration will create a pleasing, memorable sound effect. The antithesis will balance your ideas, but it will also create a conflict between two contrasting ideas. The added touch of alliteration will add an echo effect to make the sentence pack even more punch. Using an alliterative antithesis hook also opens the door for ending your composition with a smooth, satisfying conclusion.

A full-circle conclusion. As you wrap up your essay, return to your opening to give your reader the pleasing sense of coming full circle.

Directions

As you read the following passage about chewing gum, notice how the writer employs both an alliterative antithesis hook and a full-circle conclusion:

> Pick up a pack of gum; put down the stress and strain of modern life. Chewing gum is the most resourceful snack ever invented because it improves moods; more specifically it relieves anxiety, increases awareness, and reduces stress. Picture a young businesswoman multi-tasking in the hustle-bustle environment of her busy office. She's answering the phone and writing emails and completing a mound of paperwork. Unable to maintain her focus under the mounting stress, she pulls out a pack of Orbit gum and pops a piece in her mouth. Chewing the gum, she tunnels the negative energy of her stress and anxiety, burning it off rapidly. Seem hard to believe? Well, a recent study out of Swinburne University in Australia showed that participants who chewed gum in a laboratory study became more alert, more focused, and less stressed than those who went without gum. The study showed major levels of stress reduction for such a minor difference. It seems a small pack of gum packs a big punch.

1. Does the writer use an alliterative antithesis hook? Identify both the alliteration and the antithesis.
2. How does the writer connect the hook to the concluding sentence to bring the reader full-circle?
3. As a reader, how would you describe the effect of the writer's use of an alliterative antithesis hook and a full-circle conclusion?
4. Now select your own topic from a list of writing topics your teacher provides. Write an introductory paragraph that uses an alliterative antithesis hook to address the question.

Chapter 11 Teaching Notes and Answers

Additional Examples

Alliteration

Every passing week brings news for latte lovers, and the latest on coffee is the best buzz yet. —Kathleen McAuliffe

And our nation itself is testimony to the love our veterans have had for it and for us. All for which America stands is safe today because brave men and women have been ready to face the fire at freedom's front. —Ronald Reagan

When the oak is felled the whole forest echoes with its fall, but a hundred acorns are sown in silence by an unnoticed breeze. —Thomas Carlyle

Any fool can criticize, condemn, and complain—and most fools do.
—Dale Carnegie

Anaphora

To everything there is a season, and a time to every purpose under heaven:
A time to be born, and a time to die;
A time to plant, and a time to pluck up that which is planted;
A time to kill, and a time to heal;
A time to break down and a time to build up. —Ecclesiastes 3:1–3

It's not enough that the Swoosh is on Michael Jordan's beret and Mary Pierce's headband and Gabrielle Reece's beach volleyball top. It's not enough that the center on the Hawaii basketball team had his sideburns shaped into Swooshes. I want a Swoosh tattoo. I want a Swoosh lasered onto my retinas. I want to name my son Swoosh. (If it's a girl, Swooshie). —Rick Reilly.

Be sincere, be brief, be seated. —Franklin Delano Roosevelt

What we find in books is like the fire in our hearths. We fetch it from our neighbor's, we kindle it at home, we communicate it to others, and it becomes the property of all. —Voltaire

69. REPETITION FOR A REASON

Pass out the handout and have students read through the opening explanation and the examples of common phrases that use anaphora and alliteration. Next, go through the exercise, reading each item. Ask students to raise their hands if they have answers that work. Students may not recognize some of the sayings, so accept any answer as long as it makes sense and meets the definitions of either alliteration or anaphora.

Answers

Part I

1. like
2. more
3. monkey
4. news
5. no
6. nothing
7. penny
8. man's
9. fear
10. power corrupts

Part II

1. miss/mile
2. such sweet sorrow
3. practice/preach
4. proof/pudding
5. spare/spoil
6. baby/bath
7. willing/weak
8. slow/steady
9. time/tide
10. life/liberty

70. ECHOING WORDS AND SOUNDS

Give students the handout and have them read the examples and explanation relating to the effects of alliteration and anaphora. Then read aloud the example passage at the bottom of the handout about the dog. As students read and listen, they should circle examples of alliteration and anaphora. After reading the passage, discuss the use of the two techniques.

Answers

> **The one** animal that has been **d**omesticated by man without **d**iscarding its **d**ignity, **the one** animal that is **l**oyal to its master without **l**osing its independence, **the one** animal that will **s**erve without being a **s**lave is the cat. **He will** faithfully show up to be **f**ed every day but refuse to **f**ollow a schedule. **He will** approach you with elegance and grace, allowing you to **s**troke his **s**oft fur, but **he will** refuse to **b**end to **b**ase commands. **No s**aying "**s**it" to him, **no f**etching **f**lung objects. **D**rooling on **d**avenports is beneath his **d**ignity. Being **l**ed on a leash is **l**udicrous. Once deified by the Egyptians, the cat has not forgotten **his** **r**egal **r**oots, **his** imperial heritage. **He will** kill a mouse for you, but **he will** never allow you to kill his spirit.

Number of instances of alliteration: 11

Number of instances of anaphora: 5

71. RERUNS WORTH WATCHING

Consider introducing this activity by writing up an example of alliteration and an example of anaphora from the list of examples at the beginning of this chapter's "Teaching Notes and Answers." Read the examples aloud and ask students whether they notice anything special about these quotes that make them stand out. Students are more likely to recognize alliteration than anaphora, but in either case they should recognize not just what the quotations say, but also the sound of the passages. Next, give students the handout and lead them through the explanations and examples before they begin the exercise, which challenges them to recognize whether a passage contains alliteration or anaphora

Answers

1. alliteration
2. anaphora
3. alliteration
4. anaphora
5. alliteration
6. anaphora
7. alliteration

72. ONE CHANGE

Begin by brainstorming with the class possible answers to the question, "What one change would you make to improve your town, your country, or your world?" After completing a list of at least fifteen ideas, show students the handout and read the example. As students read, have them highlight uses of alliteration and anaphora. After reading, discuss the effects of these devices on the effectiveness of the writer's point. As students prepare to write their own composition, remind them of the brainstormed list along with the other requirements for the assignment.

73. OVERRATED/UNDERRATED

Before giving students the handout, write the words "overrated" and "underrated" on the board. Ask students to brainstorm a list of things that they would put under each of the two categories. After you have at least ten things under each category, pass out the handout and read the passage aloud. Ask students to circle examples of alliteration and anaphora as they listen. Next, ask students to try to articulate how the alliteration and anaphora in the passage makes it more interesting and/or memorable for the reader. As students prepare to write their own compositions, remind them of the brainstormed list. This activity should produce a variety of responses worth sharing. It also serves as a quick, formative assessment.

74. COMPOSITION REPLETE WITH REPETITIVE T'S

Pass out the handout, and read the directions together as a class. After reading the last paragraph, ask students if they noticed that every word in the directions, except for the last paragraph, contained at least one letter "t." As students write their own compositions, have them check each other's drafts to make sure that every word does in fact contain a "t." Because students can write on any topic, this activity should produce a variety of responses worth sharing.

75. ALLITERATIVE ANTITHESIS HOOK AND FULL-CIRCLE CONCLUSION

Leading students through a discussion of the three questions that follow the model will help them see the effectiveness of this strategy and prepare them to write their own paragraphs. For possible writing topics, see "101 Writing Prompts" in the "Resources" section of this book.

Possible Answers

1. Yes. The alliteration comes from the repetition of the /p/ and /s/ sounds: Pick, pack, put, stress, strain. The antithesis comes from the words "Pick up/Put down."
2. The "pack of gum" referred to in the opening sentence is repeated in the concluding sentence. Also repeated is the alliteration of the /p/ and /s/ sounds: pack, packs, punch, seems, small.
3. The alliteration and antithesis invite the reader to read the passage aloud. They give the passage a balance and an echo effect that makes it memorable.

CHAPTER **12**

Sentence Variety—The Long and the Short of It

> ## KEY TERMS
>
> **Balanced sentence:** A sentence in which the clauses are written in the same grammatical structure, such as: *Hate is a human emotion, but love is a human need.*
>
> **Cumulative sentence:** A sentence that is grammatically complete before its end, such as: *Gary played Monopoly with an intensity never before seen in any high-school cafeteria.* Sometimes called a "loose sentence."
>
> **Periodic sentence:** A sentence that is not grammatically complete until its last phrase, such as, *Despite Glenn's hatred of his sister's laziness and noisy eating habits, he still cared for her.*

THE WHAT, WHY, AND HOW OF SENTENCE VARIETY

Read the two versions of the following paragraph aloud. Which would you say is better?

Version 1

Once upon a time, any writer worth his or her salt carried a knife. Bards brandishing blades? Writers wielding weapons? Say it isn't so, Shakespeare! Well, in an age before metal-tipped pens, ballpoint pens, or typewriters, the only writing tool available was a feather—or quill. These quill pens wore down quickly. Because of this, every scribe carried a sharpening tool, a blade known as a "penknife." In fact, the word "pen" derives from the Latin word penna, meaning quill.

Version 2

Once upon a time any writer worth his or her salt carried a knife. Why would a bard brandish a knife or a writer wield a weapon? Please tell me that this legend is not true, Shakespeare! Before metal-tipped pens, the only writing tool available was a feather—or quill. Quill pens wore down quickly, so scribes carried a sharpening tool known as a "penknife." In fact, the word "pen" derives from the Latin word penna, meaning quill.

Most people pick Version 1 as the better passage. So what is the difference? The sentence variety.

Simply stated, a variety of sentence lengths and sentence structures makes for better writing. Good writing has a rhythm and resonance that rings out in the reader's ear, and the best sentences almost demand to be read aloud. In fact, one of the best ways to help students revise their writing is to have them simply read their sentences aloud. Frequently, their ears will tip them off to an off-note their eyes didn't catch.

Humans have been speaking much longer than we have been writing. Speaking is innate; writing and reading are learned skills. Our minds perk up to passages that most resemble human speech.

Now, it is certainly true that we can't write exactly like we talk; after all, much of our spoken language relies on non-verbal cues. We can, however, imitate one trait that seems to be universal in spoken language: variety in sentence length—some long, some medium, and some short. The length and types of sentences in the first passage, for example, reveal much more variety than those in the second passage. It's this variety that best simulates the sound and rhythms of human speech.

Luckily for the writer, the English sentence is made up of flexible parts that snap together like Legos of logic to construct solid, syntactical structures. Like Lego blocks, English words, phrases, and clauses allow the sentence-builder to construct an endless variety of creations: some small and simple, some large and complex, with lots of choices in-between.

The activities in this chapter will show students how variety in length and structure of sentences will make their writing more inviting, more interesting, and more pleasing to their reader's ear.

Chapter 12 Exercises

76. **Revise for Variety...Out Loud.** This activity shows students the contrast between sentences written with variety and those that are not.

77. **Sentence Smorgasbord: Cumulative and Periodic.** Two varieties of sentences deliver different kinds of rhetorical punch.

78. **I Came, I Saw, I Balanced.** Students practice a third, distinctive sentence type.

79. **What's the Difference?** Students practice writing balanced sentences, an important way to add sophistication to their syntax.

80. **Best of the Web.** Students practice writing varied sentences as they write about something of interest found on the Internet.

81. **Radio Readers.** Students apply sentence variety by writing a passage designed to be read aloud.

82. **Lessons from Fiction or Film.** Students practice composing sentences of different types and lengths as they write about a favorite book or film.

76. REVISE FOR VARIETY...OUT LOUD

Directions

Listen to the following two passages as your teacher reads them aloud to determine which is better.

Version 1

Words are like Lego building blocks. The English sentence is made up of parts. These parts snap together like Legos of logic. You can construct solid, syntactical structures. English words, phrases, and clauses come in multiple colors and forms. The sentence builder can use them to construct many creations. Some of these creations are small, some are medium, and some are large. There's no end to the fun you can have.

Version 2

Words are like Lego building blocks. The English sentence is made up of parts that snap together like Legos of logic to construct solid, syntactical structures. Like Lego blocks, English words, phrases, and clauses come in multiple colors and forms. Using these, the sentence builder may construct an infinite variety of creations: some small, some medium, and some large. There's no end to the fun you can have.

Count up the number of sentences in each of the passages and how many words are in each of the sentences of the passages.

Version 1

Total number of sentences: _____

Number of words in each sentence: _____

Version 2

Total number of sentences: _____

Number of words in each sentence: _____

77. SENTENCE SMORGASBORD: CUMULATIVE AND PERIODIC

Read the following sentences. What similarities and differences do you see?

Mary sang a song, dazzling the judges with her impressive vocal range.

Mary, who dreamed of winning the contest and traveling to Hollywood, sang a song.

The previous two sentences share the same central independent clause: Mary sang a song. In each case, though, the sentence has been expanded in different and distinctive ways. The main, independent clause begins the first sentence with the modifying information and details following it.

This type of sentence is called a *cumulative* (or loose) sentence. The cumulative sentence echoes commonly spoken language and is the most natural, informal type of sentence. For example, when you return to school after vacation, you might begin by telling your friends, "The trip was awesome." You then follow up with details that show the listener what you mean by "awesome."

Unlike the cumulative sentence, sentence 2—a *periodic* sentence—does not begin with a complete independent clause; instead, a dependent clause is wedged between the subject (*Mary*) and the verb (*sang*):

Mary, who dreamed of winning the contest and traveling to Hollywood, sang a song.

The periodic sentence has a formal, dramatic flair. Because the main idea is not complete until the end of the sentence, and because the details build suspense, the reader is left hanging until the very end.

Directions

Identify each of the following sentences as cumulative or periodic.

1. *Bill loves books: mysteries, romance novels, dictionaries, science-fiction anthologies, and how-to manuals.*

2. *Bill, who loves mysteries, romance novels, dictionaries, science-fiction anthologies, and how-to manuals, is an insatiable reader.*

3. *He walked for days, wondering what he would do when he finally arrived back where he started, his small hometown in Kansas.*

4. *Mourning his dead father, berating his clueless mother, and continually contemplating the murder of his remorseless, treacherous, and lecherous uncle, Hamlet is not having a good day!*

5. *Hamlet ruminated revenge, his anger swelling against Claudius, the illegitimate King of Denmark.*

Chapter 12 Sentence Variety—The Long and the Short of It

78. I CAME, I SAW, I BALANCED

In addition to the cumulative and periodic sentence, there is a third type of distinctive sentence that writers use. It's called a balanced sentence, and here's an example.

Mary sang a song; Bill recited a poem.

Instead of favoring one clause over another, the balanced sentence matches two or more clauses evenly. With cumulative and periodic sentences, asymmetry is used for effect; with balanced sentences, symmetry is used for that purpose. The symmetry comes by way of parallelism, the repetition of grammatical structure in a sentence. Because the two clauses follow the same pattern, they balance.

Notice how each of the following sentences maintain balance via repeated structure.

Don't worry that children never listen to you; worry that they are always watching you. —Robert Fulghum

He who sows courtesy reaps friendship, and he who plants kindness gathers love. —Saint Basil

Little minds are interested in the extraordinary; great minds in the commonplace. —Elbert Hubbard

Directions

The following four sentences are unbalanced. Revise each for balance.

1. *Jack finished in fifth place; Ron placed first.*

   _____

2. *Hate is a human emotion; humans need love.*

   _____

3. *With cumulative and periodic sentences, asymmetry is used for effect. Symmetry is used for effect with balanced sentences.*

   _____

4. *If you can't love, life has no meaning; love has no meaning, if you can't live.*

   _____

79. WHAT'S THE DIFFERENCE?

Directions

The English language enjoys a treasure trove of synonyms, words that have similar meanings but not necessarily the same *exact* meanings. Select three of the following word pairs and write three balanced sentences in which you explore the subtle differences in the meanings between the two words by providing the reader with specific examples and details.

aggressive/pushy	crowd/mob	juvenile/teen	shy/coy
angry/livid	cry/weep	late/tardy	sleep/slumber
bright/smart	energetic/hyper	laugh/giggle	student/scholar
cautious/cowardly	explorer/tourist	old/ancient	watch/gaze
criminal/thug	intelligence/wisdom	passion/zeal	wealthy/rich

Examples

Cockiness slows down when it passes a mirror; confidence slows down when it passes an attractive member of the opposite sex.

A frugal person makes prudent purchases; a miserly person pinches pennies.

80. BEST OF THE WEB

Directions

What is the single best thing on the Internet? What makes it so great? Make your case by persuading the reader with details and examples that show your point and also with varied sentences. Also include at least one cumulative, periodic, or balanced sentence.

Example

Encyclopedia Britannica *may contain enough information to cover the map of England in text, but Wikipedia contains enough information to cover both the Atlantic and Pacific Oceans. Wikipedia is the greatest thing on the Internet because it is the most comprehensive and up-to-date reference source you will ever find. Simply the largest single compilation of knowledge in the history of the human race, it dwarfs all other sources. For example, compared to* Encyclopedia Britannica's *65,000 articles, Wikipedia features nearly three million articles, and that number is growing, literally by the minute. The reason we can say "literally by the minute" is because the content on Wikipedia is constantly being updated, added to, and edited. If, for example, a celebrity dies today, chances are you'll find it reflected in that celebrity's online Wikipedia biography today! Less than two weeks after Michael Jackson's death, for example, Wikipedia featured not just a biography of Michael Jackson, but also a specific article on "The Death of Michael Jackson." This article featured more than twenty sections and 129 footnotes. There are certainly other places to find information, but nowhere will you find so much in so little time. Never have so many people been given so much information so quickly for so little cost.*

81. RADIO READERS

Directions

Write the text of a radio public-service announcement of at least 120 words in which you promote reading and/or books. Persuade your listeners to read more, or to read more to their children. Use sentence variety to give your announcement the natural sounding rhythm of human speech. Also consider including a cumulative, periodic, or balanced sentence where appropriate.

Example

It transports you across thousands of miles, sparking your imagination and lifting your soul to new heights—and all while you sit in a chair in your living room. Reading, as Emily Dickinson said, is "the frugal chariot that bears a human soul." Television is cheap, but its content is worthless; reading is inexpensive, but its content is priceless. Put down the remote, and grab a book. Open to the first page, and begin your odyssey of discovery, using your own imagination to create the pictures in your mind instead of relying on some overpaid Hollywood special-effects man. Determine your own destiny. Don't hand it over to a game-show host or some pathetic reality-show contestant. Conquer your own worlds with words, not a televised wasteland of whiners, wimps, and wannabes. Turn off your television and turn on your mind—with a book.

82. LESSONS FROM FICTION OR FILM

One of the reasons we read good books is to live vicariously through the characters' experiences. Even the lives of fictional characters have elements of truly universal experience that we can identify with and learn from. Think of a novel, play, or film that has universal truths and life lessons. Harry Potter, for example, is a wizard, but are there general human truths we can take from his books? *Star Wars* is set in a "galaxy far, far away," but it's so popular that there must be some truths in it that the citizens of Earth can learn.

Directions

Write a list of at least eight lessons. Write in complete sentences and try for a variety of sentence lengths.

Here is an example of lessons from two characters from Shakespeare.

Lessons from Romeo and Juliet

1. *Love is important, but it's not worth giving up your life for it.*
2. *Don't let your personal disagreements become a community nuisance.*
3. *Put an end to ancient grudges.*
4. *Don't crash parties thrown by life-long enemies.*
5. *Adults, as well as teenagers, can do some very stupid things.*
6. *Get to know your wife's parents before you get married.*
7. *Slow down! It's not smart to marry someone the day after you met them at party.*
8. *Try to reasonably solve major conflicts with other parties before a major, preventable tragedy happens.*

Chapter 12 Teaching Notes and Answers

76. REVISE FOR VARIETY...OUT LOUD

Give students the handout. Let them know that you will be reading two versions of the same paragraph aloud. Their mission is to decide, after listening, which passage is better.

After you read the passages, have students record their individual votes before sharing with anyone else. Next, ask individual students which passage they liked better, and then take an overall class vote. Let students know that most people pick Version 1 because its sentences have more variety. Then, have students continue to look at the handout, reading the explanations and directions contained there. They should read the two passages about how sentences are Legos and then count up the number of sentences and the number of words in each sentence. The following are the actual statistics about the two passages.

Answers
Legos

Version 1
Total number of sentences: 8
Number of words in each sentence: 6, 8, 8, 6, 11, 10, 13, 9

Version 2
Total number of sentences: 5
Number of words in each sentence: 6, 20, 14, 19, 9

Finish by making the point that a writing piece with sentences that vary in length sound pleasant to the human ear.

Penknife

Version 1
Total number of sentences: 8
Number of words in each sentence: 14, 3, 3, 5, 21, 6, 15, 13

Version 2
Total number of sentences: 6
Number of words in each sentence: 14, 13, 10, 13, 15, 13

77. SENTENCE SMORGASBORD: CUMULATIVE AND PERIODIC

To introduce this activity, put the following self-defining sentences on the board. Point out that the key difference between them is that the cumulative begins with the main clause while the periodic ends with the main clause.

The cumulative sentence is the most natural, informal type of sentence, echoing spoken language where we state a main point and support it with details.

Because the main idea is not complete until the end of the sentence, and because the details build up suspense, the periodic sentence is quite dramatic.

Give students the handout, and guide them through the two example sentences and the explanation of the difference between cumulative and periodic sentences. As students complete the activity, check their understanding by having them find the location of the main clause in each sentence. As a follow-up activity, you might have them try to transform a cumulative sentence into a periodic.

Also, use the following examples to reinforce student understanding.

Cumulative Example

Notice, for example, how Scott Russell Sanders uses a cumulative sentence to first identify one of his tools by name. He then follows the main clause with phrases that layer the details that make this hammer something special:

> *It is a finishing hammer, about the weight of a bread loaf, too light really for framing walls, too heavy for cabinetwork, with a curved claw for pulling nails, a rounded head for pounding, a fluted neck for looks, and a hickory handle for strength.*

Periodic Example

Notice how Scott Russell Sanders uses a periodic sentence to open an essay examining his relationship with both his tools and his father.

> *At just about the hour when my father died, soon after dawn one February morning when ice coated the windows like cataracts, I banged my thumb with a hammer.*

Deduction/Induction Connection

Another way to understand the difference between the cumulative and periodic sentences is by relating them to deduction and induction. The periodic sentence lends itself to inductive reasoning because it begins with showing details and ends with a central telling point.

For example, in his essay "Shooting an Elephant," George Orwell uses a periodic sentence to lead the reader inductively to his conclusion.

> *The wretched prisoners huddling in the stinking cages of the lock-ups, the gray, cowed faces of the long-term convicts, the scared buttocks of the men who had been flogged with bamboos—all these oppressed me with an intolerable sense of guilt.*

In contrast, if Orwell had been aiming for a deductive strategy, he would have selected a cumulative sentence, stating his conclusion up front.

> *All these oppressed me with an intolerable sense of guilt: the wretched prisoners huddling in the stinking cages of the lock-ups, the gray, cowed faces of the long-term convicts, the scared buttocks of the men who had been flogged with bamboos.*

Answers

1. Cumulative
2. Periodic
3. Cumulative
4. Periodic
5. Cumulative

78. I CAME, I SAW, I BALANCED

Before students try writing their own balanced sentences in this activity, make sure to lead them through the examples along with the explanation on the handout. Note: Parallelism is discussed in Chapter 9.

Answers

1. *Jack finished in fifth place; Ron finished in first place.*
2. *Hate is a human emotion; love is a human need.*
3. *With cumulative and periodic sentences, asymmetry is used for effect; with balanced sentences, symmetry is used for effect.*
4. *If you can't love, life has no meaning; if you can't live, love has no meaning.*

79. WHAT'S THE DIFFERENCE?

Before giving students the handout, write some of the synonym pairs on the board. Ask students, "Even though the words *crowd* and *mob* both refer to a collection of people, is a crowd the same thing as a mob or is there a difference?" Students might notice that the word *mob* has more negative connotations than *crowd*: that is, it suggests a disorganized, angry group.

This is a valuable discussion regarding diction—the writer's choice of words—because even though two words are synonyms they cannot always be used interchangeably. This activity challenges students to write balanced sentences, but it also has value in making them think carefully about the subtle meaning of words.

80. BEST OF THE WEB

Before students write their own compositions, read through the example passage on Wikipedia, asking students to focus on the passage's sentence variety. This passage's first sentence is a balanced sentence, the second sentence is a cumulative sentence, and the third sentence is a periodic sentence. Since this activity is near the end of the chapter, consider using it as an assessment.

81. RADIO READERS

Writing the text of a radio announcement is a natural way to assess your students' ability to apply sentence variety in their writing. A well-written announcement will sound pleasing to the ear. Have students read the example passage aloud to put this idea to the test. Then, ask students to quietly read their announcements aloud to themselves as they write them. Consider using small groups for presentations, so that everyone has an opportunity to test their announcements on an audience. This activity can serve as a quick, formative assessment of how well students understand the material in this chapter.

82. LESSONS FROM FICTION OR FILM

Before giving students the handout, lead a class discussion that asks students to identify some of the universal truths or life lessons they might draw from one of their favorite books or favorite films. Ask them to brainstorm some titles of books or films, as well as some ideas that might be drawn from those books. After students have had some time to jot down some ideas, give them the handout and read the example. The following is a list of possible topics.

Ideas for Topics

    Lessons from *Twilight*
    Lessons from *To Kill a Mockingbird*
    Lessons from *School of Rock*
    Lessons from *Monsters, Inc.*
    Lessons from *Ender's Game*
    Lessons from *Macbeth*
    Lessons from *The Lion King*

In addition to sharing their lists in small groups or with the whole class, students might publish their lists by creating posters that can be put up in class.

STYLE POINTS QUIZ

The following quiz will assess how well you understand the concepts taught in the Part 1 exercises.

1. The words *plop*, *tap*, *thud*, *scratch*, *drip*, and *dribble* are:
   A. video verbs
   B. volume verbs
   C. state of being verbs
   D. concrete nouns

2. *Duct tape is the most ingenious and versatile tool ever invented because it's vital to national security, it's a medical miracle, and it's a fashion statement.*

   The above thesis contains:

   A. one claim and one premise
   B. two claims and two premises
   C. one claim and two premises
   D. one claim and three premises

3. Which of the following sentences is written in the passive voice?
   A. *The students were happy with their test results.*
   B. *The tests were handed back to the students.*
   C. *The teacher handed the tests back to the students.*
   D. *The students examined their tests.*

4. *As his relationship with the girl continued, he fell madly in love and deeper in debt.*

   The above sentence is an example of:

   A. *passive voice*
   B. *a simile*
   C. *zeugma*
   D. *personification*

5. *Kindness is the language which the deaf can hear and the blind can see.*
   —Mark Twain

   The above sentence contains:

   A. a metaphor
   B. an allusion
   C. personification
   D. a hyphenated modifier

6. Which of the following lists of words is arranged so that it begins with the most general idea and ends with the most specific idea?
   A. money, coins, the economy, finances
   B. coins, money, finances, the economy
   C. the economy, finances, money, coins,
   D. finances, the economy, money, coins

7. Read the following three sentences carefully and choose the best answer.

   I. *A frugal person makes prudent purchases; a miserly person pinches pennies.*

   II. *He walked for days, wondering what he would do when he finally arrived back where he started, his small hometown in Kansas.*

   III. *Bill, who loves mysteries, romance novels, dictionaries, science-fiction anthologies, and how-to manuals, is an insatiable reader.*

   A. Sentence I is a cumulative sentence, II is a periodic sentence, and III is a balanced sentence.

   B. Sentence I is a periodic sentence, II is a cumulative sentence, and III is a balanced sentence.

   C. Sentence I is a balanced sentence, II is a periodic sentence, and III is a cumulative sentence.

   D. Sentence I is a balanced sentence, II is a cumulative sentence, and III is a periodic sentence.

8. Based on the following two groups of words, which statement is true?

   I. *dog, rain, table, shoulder*

   II. *fear, success, joy, truth*

   A. Group I is abstract nouns and Group II is concrete nouns.

   B. Group I is concrete nouns and Group II is abstract nouns.

   C. Group I is abstract nouns and Group II is video verbs.

   D. Group I is concrete nouns and Group II is volume verbs.

9. Based on the following three sentences, which statement is true?

   I. *I went to the store and bought apples, oranges, bananas, grapes.*

   II. *I went to the store and bought apples and oranges and bananas.*

   III. *I went to the store and bought apples, oranges, and bananas.*

   A. Sentence I is written using asyndeton and Sentence II is written using polysyndeton.

   B. Sentence II is written using asyndeton and Sentence I is written using polysyndeton.

   C. Sentence I is written using asyndeton and Sentence III is written using polysyndeton.

   D. Sentence II is written using asyndeton and Sentence III is written using polysyndeton.

10. *She's one of those I-haven't-read-anything-but-a-Harry-Potter-book-in-five-years students.*

   The above sentence contains:

   A. a metaphor

   B. a simile

   C. personification

   D. a hyphenated modifier

11. *You can't hit a home run unless you step up to the plate. You can't catch fish unless you put your line in the water. You can't reach your goals if you don't try.*

    Which is true about this quote?

    A. It is inductive, moving from specific to general details.
    B. It is deductive, moving from specific to general details.
    C. It is inductive, moving from general to specific details.
    D. It is deductive, moving from general to specific details.

12. *Limited vocabulary, like short legs on a pole-vaulter, builds in a natural barrier to progress beyond a certain point.* —John Gardner

    The above sentence contains:

    A. a metaphor
    B. a simile
    C. personification
    D. a hyphenated modifier

13. *He that hath wife and children hath given hostages to fortune.* —Francis Bacon

    The above sentence contains:

    A. a metaphor
    B. a simile
    C. personification
    D. a hyphenated modifier

14. Which of the following groups of words are state-of-being verbs?

    A. *is, am, was, were, being*
    B. *stroll, walk, glare, look*
    C. *clog, scramble, crush, swoon*
    D. *whistle, slurp, flap, splash*

15. *Language is the Rubicon that divides man from beast.* —Max Muller

    The above sentence contains:

    A. a simile
    B. an allusion
    C. personification
    D. a hyphenated modifier

16. *To get profit without risk, experience without danger, and reward without work is as impossible as it is to live without being born.* —A.P. Gouthey

    The above sentence contains:

    A. allusion
    B. personification
    C. parallelism
    D. zeugma

17. *Some men see things as they are and say, "Why?" I dream things that never were and say, "Why not?"* —Robert F. Kennedy

    The above sentence contains:

    A. allusion

    B. hyphenated modifier

    C. personification

    D. antithesis

18. *And our nation itself is testimony to the love our veterans have had for it and for us. All for which America stands is safe today because brave men and women have been ready to face the fire at freedom's front.* —Ronald Reagan

    The above sentence contains:

    A. alliteration

    B. hyphenated modifier

    C. personification

    D. allusion

19. *We can learn much from wise words, little from wisecracks, and less from wise guys.* —William Arthur Ward

    This quote shows:

    A. anaphora

    B. simile

    C. allusion

    D. personification

20. The words *applaud, drag, embrace, snatch, plead,* and *survey* are:

    A. state-of-being verbs

    B. volume verbs

    C. video verbs

    D. concrete nouns

Style Points Quiz Answers

After students have taken the quiz individually, go through each problem in class to clarify each answer. As you discuss the questions, you might ask students to not just give their answers, but to also to explain why they chose those answers, justifying them based on definitions and the specific language in the test item.

1. B
2. D
3. B
4. C
5. A
6. C
7. E
8. B
9. A
10. D
11. A
12. B
13. C
14. A
15. B
16. C
17. D
18. A
19. A
20. C

PART II

Putting the Essay Together

After completing Part I of this book, students are prepared to begin applying the exercises in essays. The chapters that follow are designed to help you guide students through the writing process and apply the points they have learned as they plan, draft, revise, and edit fully developed essays.

You can require students to hand in their completed worksheets and drafts for formal assessment, or formally assess only the final draft. Either way, make sure the students use the worksheets for support as they move through the writing process. Expect the following three steps explained to take up about three to five days of instruction.

CHAPTER 13

Guiding Students through the Writing Process

STEP 1: PRE-WRITING AND WRITING A CONCLUSION AND THE FIRST DRAFT

Once the essay questions have been chosen or assigned, students should spend some time brainstorming ideas before they begin their first drafts. This type of pre-writing will help them find their point—their thesis—and force them to think about specific examples they can use to support it. It will also help them to anticipate possible objections to their reasons and examples, strengthening arguments that will persuade skeptical readers.

Any truly argumentative question will have two sides—that is, after all, what makes it a matter worth arguing. For example, if one person feels that Abraham Lincoln is the greatest American president of all time, someone else might have reasons to argue that this is not a valid claim. Likewise, if one person claims that the death penalty should remain legal, an opposing claim would state that it should not remain legal.

Whichever questions students are writing about, have them break them into these two sides. Explain that they need to look at both sides of each question because even though they may come down on one side, their reader may not. As students will remember if they did the activity "Build Your Ethos with Counterarguments" in Chapter 1, the strongest arguments don't focus on just one side. Instead, they anticipate and answer possible objections.

Topic. Begin by selecting a writing prompt from "101 Writing Prompts" in the "Resources" section at the back of this book. Instead of assigning one topic, you can tell students they can choose from a few select topics or allow students to pick any topic they want (all are suitable for persuasive essays).

Pre-writing. Once students have a writing topic, guide them through the "Pre-writing for a Point" activity explained in this section. Completing this sheet will help students look at both sides of the question and support them as they begin outlining ideas that will make solid, persuasive essays. Before students complete the "Pre-writing for a Point" chart on their own topic, you might consider selecting a topic for the whole class or small groups to work on as a model. This gives them an opportunity to practice the format and put their heads together to generate ideas.

After writing down their questions, students then break each into two groups: one for the topic and one against. They then should begin generating possible premises (reasons), examples, and details that might be used to support each side. See an example of a model, the completed "Pre-writing for a Point" chart on p. 195. The activity takes an entire class period. Once they have completed this portion of the activities, they can then complete first drafts of their essays for homework or during the next class period.

Writing the first draft. Once students have completed filling out the columns on both sides of their questions, ask them to take a careful look at which side of the argument has the most persuasive reasons and evidence. Once they decide, they are ready to draft their thesis and begin the first draft of their essays.

Remind them to focus on ideas and details over any other aspects of style as they write their first drafts. By focusing on ideas and details while drafting, students will produce well-supported drafts that will provide a solid foundation upon which to build during the revision process.

Opening hooks review. Strategies for opening an essay are covered in Chapter 2 (inductive hook), Chapter 4 (concrete noun hook), Chapter 6 (figurative language hook), and Chapter 11 (alliterative antithesis hook). Remind students that they will want to select one of these strategies to make a strong first impression with their readers.

Conclusion. Begin the next activity, "Conclusions: How Does it All End?," by asking students what advice they would give someone who asked them how to write an effective concluding paragraph to an essay. After they have offered a few ideas, give them the handout and read through the opening paragraph. You might ask them if it is true that sometimes "students just tack on a concluding paragraph."

Let them know that this activity will give them a strategy for crafting a conclusion that will make their essays clearer and more complete. Read through the explanations of the two steps, and then have students write their own concluding paragraph by either revising a past concluding paragraph or by writing one based on an essay they are currently writing. This activity will also take about one class period.

PRE-WRITING FOR A POINT: STUDENT SCAFFOLD

Name: _____

Question: _____

_____

YES:	NO:
Reason and Example 1	**Reason and Example 1**
Reason and Example 2	**Reason and Example 2**
Reason and Example 3	**Reason and Example 3**

Chapter 13 Guiding Students through the Writing Process

CONCLUSIONS: HOW DOES IT ALL END?

Don't underestimate the value of a strong finish. It's the last impression you make with your audience, and your last—and probably best—chance to make your point memorable. Follow the two steps explained below to craft a compelling concluding paragraph.

I. Rephrase rather than repeat. The conclusion reminds the reader of your main point, but it never just repeats or restates the thesis using the same words. Instead, rephrase your thesis.

Example

Original: *Duct tape is the most ingenious and versatile tool ever invented because it's vital to national security, it's a medical miracle, and it's a fashion statement.*

Rephrased: *Your security, your health, and the clothes on your back all serve to illustrate the amazing wonder that is duct tape.*

II. Use a clincher. You can use one of the following two techniques to rephrase the final sentences of your conclusion and clinch the reader's attention.

1. Anaphora clincher. You want your point to echo in the mind of your reader long after reading your composition, so why not use the echo effect of anaphora? This is nothing new; the last words of great speeches from the past still echo in our ears today.

Free at last. Free at last. Thank God Almighty, we are free at last.
—Martin Luther King

I know not what course others may take; but as for me, give me liberty or give me death! —Patrick Henry

2. Full-circle clincher. If you began your piece with an example or anecdote, end by making a reference back to those details. If you began with concrete nouns or a metaphor, take the reader back to those opening images. If you used alliteration and antithesis in your opening, repeat those contrasting, alliterative words in your closing. Any of these techniques will bring your reader full-circle and thus will bring your composition to a sensible, satisfying, and smooth close.

Directions

Take the concluding paragraph of an essay you have written, or are now writing, and write a concluding paragraph that features a rephrased thesis and an anaphora or full-circle clincher.

STEP 2: REVISING FOR COHERENCE AND ORGANIZATION

Targeted revision. Once students have a complete first draft, turn to the section "Helping Students Revise for Coherence and Organization." Before students revise their own drafts, take them through the activity called "Keeping It Coherent," during which they will analyze two different versions of an essay for transitions. This activity provides strategies for using transitions within and between sentences and between paragraphs and will take a complete class period.

Next, students will look at their own first drafts and begin revising for coherence. If time permits, have them complete second drafts of their essays in which they focus on coherence and include a strong opening hook, a solid conclusion, and effective transitions between paragraphs.

Self-revision and peer revision. Revising continues as you give out copies of the student handout "Review and Revision Reminders" found in the "Resources" section. This sheet summarizes all the writing strategies they have learned and serves as a reminder of each strategy they can use as they revise and provide feedback to their peers. Students continue revising using a checklist. "Pointing the Way—Self-revision and Peer Revision" helps students improve their own essays and provide constructive feedback to their peers using a step-by-step approach.

After their essays have been analyzed with the self-revision and peer-revision sheet, students can continue to use the "Review and Revision Reminders" handout for ideas to improve essays as they write their third drafts.

By now, students should have realized that it is the writer's responsibility to build continuity into his or her writing, which helps the reader follow the writer's train of thought from sentence to sentence and from paragraph to paragraph. This continuity is called coherence.

As students revise their first and second drafts, it is important to address the coherence of the essays. In other words, is the essay organized so that the reader is led through the beginning, middle, and end in a smooth and clear manner?

Lead students through the activities in the handouts "Signal Words: Three Techniques for Coherent Writing" and "Keeping It Coherent," and refer to the teaching notes following the chapter for additional instructional tips.

KEEPING IT COHERENT: COMPARING ESSAYS

The following two versions of the same essay were written on the following question:

What is the single best thing on the Internet? What makes it so great?

Read both versions with the following question in mind:

Which essay does a better job of moving the reader smoothly from point to point?

When you have identified the essay, try to identify how the writer does this by highlighting at least three places in the essay where the writer signals and links ideas.

Version A

In today's modern world there are so many resources available on the World Wide Web, but one stands out from the crowd. Without a doubt, Wikipedia is the single best thing on the Internet because it is quick and easy to use, because it is comprehensive and up-to-date, and because it is democratic.

The reason Wikipedia is great is because it has taken the time element out of reference work because it is so quick and easy to use. No trips to the library, no lugging around encyclopedias, no searching through indexes for the right article. Suppose, for example, you are reading a novel and come across an unfamiliar reference, such as the expression "hoist with one's own petard." Just type in the expression into your search engine followed by the word "wiki" and you'll instantly be transported on the information superhighway to the appropriate Wikipedia article. In a flash you will learn that this expression originates from the French language and dates from the 16th century. It means "to fall into one's own trap." If you have a little more time to read, you'll learn that Shakespeare popularized the expression in his play Hamlet, it means "firecracker" in modern French slang, and, oddly, it has a historic connection to a Latin term for flatulence.

The second reason Wikipedia is great is because it is also the most comprehensive and up-to-date reference source you'll ever find. Wikipedia is simply the largest single compilation of knowledge in the history of the human race. It dwarfs all other sources. For example, compared to Encyclopedia Britannica's 65,000 articles, Wikipedia features nearly three million articles, and that number is growing, literally by the minute. The reason we can say "literally by the minute" is because the content on Wikipedia is constantly being updated, added to, and edited. If, for example, a celebrity dies today, chances are you'll find it reflected in that celebrity's online Wikipedia biography today! Less than two weeks after Michael Jackson's death, for example, Wikipedia featured not just a biography of Michael Jackson but also a specific article on "The Death of Michael Jackson." This article featured more than twenty sections and 129 footnotes.

The third reason that Wikipedia is great is because its content is free and open to everyone. It's the most democratic of all sources. Approximately 65 million people around the world access Wikipedia each month and more than 75,000 people have contributed content. Anyone can access, contribute, or edit Wikipedia articles, and there is no distracting advertising. Like a community garden, anyone can come to Wikipedia's fertile soil of knowledge. Many hands like light work, and as the content grows thousands of wiki gardeners plant, weed, and water the planting beds. And if a vandal comes on the scene, many eyes are watching, and even if some damage is done, there are thousands ready to pitch in to clean up any mess.

Some people are not impressed with Wikipedia. The true problem here, however, is not Wikipedia, but simply the misuse of the online encyclopedia. Unlike reviewed, published sources, Wikipedia is an "open source." Because anyone can contribute to Wikipedia, not everything found there meets the standards of serious scholarly research. Even Wikipedia's founder, Jimmy Wales, explains that students can use it for getting background information on a topic, but that it is not the kinds of source that should be cited in academic writing or other serious research. Wikipedia is a tool that students should use in appropriate contexts; if you have a nail that needs to be pounded, use a hammer, not a screwdriver. Misuse of the Wikipedia tool doesn't diminish the value of this sledgehammer of the information superhighway, but it is a reminder that students need to be instructed on its proper use. You wouldn't want your doctor, for example, searching for medical information on Wikipedia before he operates on you.

Wikipedia is the 21st century's greatest information source. Its speed, ease of use, timeliness, enormous content, and democratic nature make it worth celebrating. So mark your calendar today and start planning ahead for this year's Wikipedia Day on January 15th.

Version B

Some people believe that the 21st century began on January 1, 2001, but the truth is it didn't actually begin until January 15th of that year. On this date, the world was opened up to a new universe of information. On this date, Wikipedia, the free Internet encyclopedia, went online for the first time. Without a doubt, Wikipedia is the single best thing on the Internet because it is quick and easy to use, because it is comprehensive and up-to-date, and because it is democratic. You can mark January 15th on your calendar now and begin planning your own Wikipedia Day party; the truth is, however, every day is Wikipedia Day.

No Wikipedia Day party is complete without a few Hawaiian decorations. Why Hawaiian? Because the word "wiki" comes from the Hawaiian word for "quick." Wikipedia has taken the time element out of reference work because it is so quick and easy to use. No trips to the library, no lugging around encyclopedias, no searching through indexes for the right article. Suppose, for example, you are reading a novel and come across an unfamiliar reference, such as the expression "hoist with one's own petard." Just type the expression into your search engine followed by the word "wiki" and you'll instantly be transported on the information superhighway to the appropriate Wikipedia article. In a flash you will learn that this expression originates from French and dates from the 16th century. It means "to fall into one's own trap." If you have a little more time to read, you'll learn that Shakespeare popularized the expression in his play Hamlet, it means "firecracker" in modern French slang, and, oddly, it has a historic connection to a Latin term for flatulence. Where else can you find so much information so easily and in so little time?

Ease of use and saving time are not the only reasons to celebrate, however. Wikipedia is also the most comprehensive and up-to-date reference source you'll ever find. Wikipedia is simply the largest single compilation of knowledge in the history of the human race. It dwarfs all other sources. For example, compared to Encyclopedia Britannica's 65,000 articles, Wikipedia features nearly three million articles, and that number is growing, literally by the minute. The reason we can say "literally by the minute" is because the content on Wikipedia is constantly being updated, added to, and edited. If, for example, a celebrity dies today, chances are you'll find it reflected in that celebrity's online Wikipedia biography today! Less than two weeks after Michael Jackson's death, for example, Wikipedia featured not just a biography of Michael Jackson, but also a specific article on "The Death of Michael Jackson." This article featured more than twenty sections and 129 footnotes. There are certainly other places to find information, but nowhere will you find so much in so little time.

Never have so many people been given so much information for so little cost. The content of Wikipedia is free and open to everyone. It's the most democratic of all sources. Approximately 65 million people around the world access Wikipedia each month and more than 75,000 people have contributed content. Anyone can access, contribute, or edit Wikipedia articles, and there is no distracting advertising. Like a community garden, anyone can come to Wikipedia's fertile soil of knowledge. Many hands like light work, and as the content grows, thousands of wiki gardeners plant, weed, and water the planting beds. And if a vandal comes on the scene, there are many eyes watching, and even if some damage is done, there are thousands ready to pitch in to clean up the mess.

To be fair, while some see Wikipedia as a garden, others see it as a festering cesspool. The true problem here, however, is not Wikipedia but simply the misuse of the online encyclopedia. Unlike reviewed, published sources, Wikipedia is an "open source"; this means that anyone can contribute to Wikipedia, so not everything found there meets the standards of serious scholarly research. Even Wikipedia's founder, Jimmy Wales, explains that students can use it for getting background information on a topic, but that it is not the kind of source that should be cited in academic writing or other serious research. Wikipedia is a tool that students should use in appropriate contexts; if you have a nail that needs to be pounded, use a hammer, not a screwdriver. Misuse of the Wikipedia tool doesn't diminish the value of this sledgehammer of the information superhighway, but it is a reminder that students need to be instructed on its proper use. You wouldn't want your doctor, for example, searching for medical information on Wikipedia before he operates on you.

The misuse of Wikipedia by some should not damper enthusiasm for the positive aspects of the 21st century's greatest information source. Its speed, ease of use, timeliness, enormous content, and democratic nature make it worth celebrating. So mark your calendar today and start planning ahead for this year's Wikipedia Day on January 15th.

SIGNAL WORDS:
THREE TECHNIQUES FOR COHERENT WRITING

The three techniques that follow are the most valuable tools for coherent writing.

Repetition. Writers repeat words and ideas to guide the reader within a single sentence and between sentences and paragraphs. Repeating a word or phrase between sentences links the sentences, coupling ideas and keeping the reader on track. Repetition is also an excellent way to transition from one paragraph to another. You can, for example, repeat an idea from the previous paragraph before you present a new idea in the next one. The paragraphs are linked, and the reader moves smoothly and seamlessly through the essay.

Pronouns and synonyms. Repetition is a useful way to link ideas, but too much can create problems. After all, readers like variety. The solution is using pronouns (for example, *it, they, his*) and synonyms. Pronouns save space and save the reader from reading the same word over and over. Likewise, the rich variety of synonyms in English invites writers to use a different word for the same idea. A synonym is a great option to avoid reader boredom. Like repetition, pronouns and synonyms link ideas within a sentence and between them.

Transition words. Transition words are the GPS of the writing world. They keep the reader oriented within a sentence and between sentences and reveal the relationship between ideas. Transition words are often overlooked. Great writers, however, know that they are vital tools for keeping writing logical and coherent.

The following table lists some of the various transition words that show different types of logical connections.

Transition Words

TYPE OF LOGICAL CONNECTION	EXAMPLES
Addition	*another, and, also, in addition*
Compare and contrast	*but, however, although, yet, nevertheless, even though, on the other hand, similarly, likewise, in the same way*
Place/Location	*on, over, under, above, below, next to, inside, outside, adjacent to*
Example/Illustration	*for example, for instance, such as, specifically, to demonstrate, to illustrate*
Cause and effect	*because, if, therefore, so, as a result, thus*
Time or sequence	*first, second, third, next, before, after, then, finally, meanwhile*
Emphasis or summary	*in fact, again, to repeat, in other words*

POINTING THE WAY: SELF REVISION AND PEER REVISION

Name of Writer: _____

Name of Peer Reviewer: _____

Ideas and Details that are Cogent and Credible

1. Claims and premises: What is the writer's thesis?

    _____

2. Is the thesis clear and concise?

    Yes _____ No _____

3. Does the thesis include both the writer's claim and the writer's premises?

    Yes _____ No _____

4. Does the writer use any counterarguments?

    Yes _____ No _____

5. Examples and anecdotes: Does the writer use specific examples and anecdotes that show rather than just tell?

    Yes _____ No _____

Diction that Is Concrete and Concise

1. Vivid Verbs: Does the writer use plenty of specific, vivid verbs?

    Yes _____ No _____

    If yes, give four examples:

    _____

2. Concrete Nouns: Does the writer use plenty of concrete nouns from the bottom rung of the Ladder of Abstraction?

    Yes _____ No _____

    If yes, give four examples:

    _____

3. Lists (asyndeton/polysyndeton): Does the writer use any lists?

Yes _____ No _____

If yes, give an examples:

_____

4. Zeugma: Does the writer use zeugma?

Yes _____ No _____

If yes, give an examples:

_____

5. Hyphenated Modifier: Does the writer use any hyphenated modifiers?

Yes _____ No _____

If yes, give an examples:

_____

Voice and Figurative Language that is Compelling and Creative

1. Does the writer use metaphors, similes, personification, or allusions?

Yes _____ No _____

If yes, which ones (circle):

Metaphors   Similes   Personification   Allusions

Syntax that is Clear and Correct

1. Is there a variety in the length, openings, and structure of sentences?

Yes _____ No _____

2. Does the writer use parallelism?

Yes _____ No _____

If yes, give an examples:

_____

3. Does the writer use antithesis?

Yes _____ No _____

If yes, give an examples:

_____

4. Does the writer use anaphora?

Yes _____ No _____

If yes, give an examples:

_____

5. Does the writer use alliteration?

Yes _____ No _____

If yes, give an examples:

_____

Organization that is Coherent and Complete

1. Does the writer use an opening hook?

Yes _____ No _____

If yes, which type (circle one):

Inductive   Concrete   Metaphor   Alliterative Antithesis

2. Does the writer conclude by rephrasing the thesis?

Yes _____ No _____

3. Does the writer include a clincher in the concluding paragraph?

Yes _____ No _____

If yes, which type (circle one):

Full circle   Anaphora

4. Does the writer use signal words to move smoothly through the paper and between paragraphs? (Look for transition words, repeated words, and synonyms and pronouns.)

Yes _____   No _____

STEP 3: EDITING FOR THE CORRECT USE OF CONVENTIONS

Editing for conventions is the final step in the essay-writing process. Students use the "Editing Checklist" to remind them of specific errors to look for in grammar, punctuation, and mechanics.

Allow some time in class for students to use the checklist to edit their essays and those of their peers. After editing for conventions, students are now ready to write their fourth and final drafts, which they will hand in for formal assessment.

EDITING CHECKLIST

Proofreading and editing for conventions are the writer's responsibility. Read your paper aloud to catch problems you might not otherwise notice. Also, use the following questions as reminders of what to look for as you edit.

Grammar

1. _____ Are there any run-on sentences or fragments?

2. _____ Do the subjects agree with the verbs?

3. _____ Are pronouns used correctly?

4. _____ Are adjectives and adverbs used correctly?

5. _____ Is the verb tense consistent?

6. _____ Is the point of view consistent?

7. _____ Are sentences clear and free of unnecessary words?

Punctuation

8. _____ Are commas used correctly?

9. _____ Are quotation marks used correctly?

10. _____ Are semicolons and colons used correctly?

11. _____ Are apostrophes used correctly?

12. _____ Are end punctuation marks (periods, exclamation marks, and question marks) used correctly?

Mechanics

13. _____ Are words spelled correctly?

14. _____ Are the rules of capitalization followed?

15. _____ Are abbreviations and numbers written correctly?

16. _____ Are titles correctly formatted?

Chapter 13 Teaching Notes

PRE-WRITING FOR A POINT

The first time you do this activity with students, do it as a whole-class or small-group activity so that students can collaborate to generate more variety of reasons and examples. Give students a copy of the "Pre-writing for a Point" form and select a specific question for them to complete (if you need a question, see "101 Writing Prompts" in the "Resources" section in this book). Let students know that they are looking at both sides of the question so that they will be prepared to anticipate their reader's possible objections. Remind them of the activity from Chapter 1 on counterarguments.

The following is an example of a completed form on the topic of the death penalty.

Question: Should the death penalty remain legal in the U.S.? Why or why not?

YES: KEEP THE DEATH PENALTY LEGAL	NO: OUTLAW THE DEATH PENALTY
Reason and Example 1 The only just punishment for murder is death. Historical precedence and the great philosophical minds throughout history testify to the appropriateness of the death penalty.	**Reason and Example 1** The death penalty does not deter crime. Statistics show that states that have a death penalty have even higher crime rates than those that have outlawed the death penalty.
Reason and Example 2 It is constitutional. The death penalty can be administered using methods that make it neither "cruel" nor "unusual."*	**Reason and Example 2** It is unconstitutional because it is "cruel and unusual punishment." Even new, supposedly humane methods have caused excessive pain and suffering to the victim.
Reason and Example 3 The death penalty prevents future victims and saves money. A murderer who is put to death will never kill another innocent victim. Likewise, the state will save the millions of dollars required to house, feed, clothe, and pay for the legal fees of convicted killers.	**Reason and Example 3** It is irrevocable. Recent cases of people released from death row because of DNA evidence show that even years after a crime has been committed, a convicted person can be exonerated by new evidence.

Once students have shared their answers, either with the entire class or in small groups, have them practice using information from the form to write possible thesis statements. For example, using information from the above form on the death penalty, a student might write the following thesis:

> *The death penalty should remain legal because it is constitutional, it is a just punishment for murder, and it prevents the future death of innocent victims.*

CONCLUSIONS: HOW DOES IT ALL END?

The three-step process explained in this activity will give students a specific strategy for writing a solid concluding paragraph. Emphasize both rephrasing the thesis and using either a full-circle or an anaphora clincher. As students write concluding paragraphs, have them share and check their revisions with a partner. Instruct them to look at the writer's original thesis and compare it with the rephrased thesis in the concluding paragraph. Also, have them see whether they can determine which type of clincher was used.

KEEPING IT COHERENT: COMPARING ESSAYS

The two versions of the essay were written to answer the following question: What is the single best thing on the Internet? What makes it so great?

Hand out the essays for individual or small group work. Students should read both versions with the following question in mind: Which essay does the better job of moving you, the reader, smoothly from point to point?

If students are working alone or in groups, they should choose what they consider to be the better essay and circle or highlight at least three places where the writer links ideas or moves the essay along. If you project the essays, circle or highlight at least three signal words of transitions together with the class as you discuss the techniques.

SIGNAL WORDS:
THREE TECHNIQUES FOR COHERENT WRITING

After students have read the two versions, hold a class discussion, calling on students to explain which version was more coherent. Students will probably select Version B because of how it uses signal words and transitions.

After students have shared, give them the student handout "Signal Words: Three Techniques for Coherent Writing." Students should highlight or circle specific examples of signal words (transition words, repetition, synonyms, and pronouns) from Version B. Also, point out the words the writer used to make smooth transitions between paragraphs, and contrast them with Version A's choppy transitions.

Last, students should refer to their drafts and revise for signal words and transitions that will link their ideas and move the reader smoothly from the beginning to the end.

POINTING THE WAY: SELF REVISION AND PEER REVISION

Students should use this form to guide them in either self revision or peer revision. Once students have a complete draft of an essay, give them the form. If they are doing peer revision, have them work in pairs to revise each other's essays. This form will give students an extensive list of specific things to look for as they do self revision and peer revision. Let them know that the purpose of filling out the form is not to grade the essay. Instead, the purpose is to help the writer of the essay to find possible areas in the essay that might be improved during revision. Furthermore, let students know that the purpose of the "yes/no" format is to suggest possibilities. Because the form requires students to do a careful, detailed reading, give them an entire period to complete it. For students working on peer revision, consider giving them some time to meet with each other to read and discuss each other's revisions.

EDITING CHECKLIST

Give students a copy of this checklist and have them use it during the editing process of their own essays or for peer editing.

CHAPTER **14**

Problem-solving and Assessment

This chapter will give you ideas on how to fit the style points into your existing writing program, using existing rubrics and writing assessment criteria. It also provides model essays and a six-point writing rubric that you can give to students in order to demystify writing assessment.

PINPOINTING PROBLEMS: MATCHING RUBRICS WITH THE STRATEGIES

You can teach the style points sequentially, but you can also customize the strategies based on your students' strengths and weaknesses. Use the following explanations to help you match up whatever writing rubrics or writing criteria you use with the style point strategies and lessons.

Ideas and Details

Good writing is cogent and credible. It contains a clear point that is supported by showing evidence. The writers are responsible for stating what their point is, telling why it is true, and showing how it is true with valid, credible evidence and details.

Claims and premises. Reviewing Chapter 1 will help students understand the importance of a clear, logical thesis, not just to give them direction in writing, but also to give their reader direction in reading. In addition, counterarguments are addressed to help students examine both sides of an issue.

Examples, anecdotes, statistics, quotations, and dialogue. Reviewing Chapter 2 will help students understand the importance of going beyond telling, to showing with concrete, detailed evidence.

Persuasive appeals. Reviewing Chapter 2 will give students an introduction to three methods of persuasion that date back to ancient Greece: logos, ethos, and pathos.

Diction (Word Choice)

Good writing is made up of language that is concrete and concise. Understanding how to select words that paint sensory pictures for the reader will help students develop a writing style that is more distinctive and more detailed.

Vivid verbs and zeugma. Reviewing Chapter 3 will help students understand how verbs invoke both sight and sound. They will learn that not every verb is the same and the importance of being discriminating in their selection of verbs.

Concrete nouns. Reviewing Chapter 4 will introduce students to the Ladder of Abstraction, a powerful tool for visualizing the way words range from abstract to concrete. They'll see the importance of selecting concrete nouns from the bottom rung.

Lists (asyndeton and polysyndeton) and hyphenated modifiers. Reviewing Chapter 5 will give students new ways to incorporate concrete word choice into their writing. They'll learn how making small changes in a sentence can make a big difference.

Voice and Figurative Language

Good writing is compelling and creative. Using the style points categorized under figurative language and repetition, students will acquire the tools they need to develop their own individual and distinctive voices. Practicing these strategies will allow students to write using vivid images, fresh insights, and resonant language.

Metaphors and similes. Reviewing Chapter 6 will introduce students to these powerful strategies for making even the blandest topic fresh and interesting.

Personification. Reviewing Chapter 7 will give students another powerful strategy for literally bringing life to their words.

Allusion. Reviewing Chapter 8 will teach students about a strategy that combines the power of story with the power of metaphor. Connecting their ideas to timeless stories from mythology, literature, and history will give students' voices a variety of distinctive tones.

Syntax and Sentence Fluency

Good writing is clear and correct. Learning to focus on sentence variety and practicing parallelism will help students craft sentences so resonant that they demand to be read aloud.

Parallelism. Reviewing Chapter 9 will put a powerful tool in the hands of students—a tool that allows students to craft sentences that are packed with ideas, rhythm, and clarity.

Antithesis. Reviewing Chapter 10 will demonstrate for students the power of balancing opposing ideas with antithesis. Students will learn that when ideas clash, readers stay interested.

Alliteration and anaphora. Reviewing Chapter 11 will equip students with two powerful strategies for balancing both sound and sense. These rhetorical reruns will give student writing eloquence, emphasis, and energy.

Sentence length and variety. Reviewing Chapter 12 will give students sentence-writing strategies for making their writing sound more natural, rhythmic, and interesting. It will also introduce students to three distinctive varieties of sentences: periodic, cumulative, and balanced.

Organization

Good writing is coherent and complete. It has a beginning, a middle, and an end, and good writers consider the importance of each part. In addition, addressing their beginnings and endings will help students learn to start strong and finish with flash. Another vital element in organization is moving the reader smoothly from beginning to end, especially from sentence to sentence and from paragraph to paragraph. Chapters 1 and 13 provide three key methods for signaling the reader.

Opening hooks. Four strategies for writing introductions will give students invaluable tools for capturing their reader's attention from the first sentence.

Inductive hook: Chapter 2
Concrete noun hook: Chapter 4
Figurative-language hook: Chapter 6
Alliterative antithesis hook: Chapter 11

Conclusions. Chapter 13 teaches a strategy for writing concluding paragraphs by rephrasing the thesis and ending with a clincher.

Deductive and inductive organization. An activity in Chapter 2 explains the difference between organizing from the general to the specific and from the specific to the general.

SCORING ESSAYS WITH A RUBRIC

Using a scoring rubric like the one presented in this chapter helps both the teacher and student in their pursuit of excellence in writing.

For the teacher, a rubric allows the consistent scoring of papers using clear, set criteria. Grading, therefore, becomes less capricious and more precise. As the teacher becomes more comfortable with the rubric's criteria, essay scoring also takes less time. Drawing language directly from the rubric for comments, for example, will allow the teacher to pinpoint feedback to the specific writing level laid out by the rubric.

For the student, a rubric demystifies the evaluation process. Because the criteria are laid out clearly, students can reach to achieve the highest level. If they don't achieve, they understand by looking at the rubric what they need to do to improve.

Students should be given the rubric and should practice scoring essays written by others as well as their own. Using the rubric will allow students to become comfortable and confident with the standards for excellence in writing. It will also allow them to more consistently reach the highest levels in their own writing. Armed with the tool chest of strategy points they learn in this book, students will begin to see how applying them in their essays will help them to reach high scores consistently.

Refer to "Teaching Notes" at the end of this chapter for additional instructional information.

Essay Scoring with a Rubric: After a class discussion, students read and score three practice essays about goal setting.

Rubric: The following six-point rubric can be used holistically; that is, giving a paper a single score (1 through 6) along with specific comments. Because it describes specific criteria in different categories (Ideas, Organization, Word Choice, Voice, Sentence Structure/Conventions), the rubric can also be used to score individual traits.

Scoring Essays with a Rubric

The following three essays are all responses to the prompt "What one thing would you say is overrated? Why?"

Read each essay carefully. Then, using the Six-point Writing Rubric, score the essay from 1 to 6 based on the rubric's criteria. To justify your score, write comments that tie the essay's content to the rubric's criteria.

Version A

Many people see goals as important tools for achieving success, but there is actually a dark side to goal setting that brings about an undesirable effect. Goal setting is not necessarily a bad thing, but it is overrated. This is because sometimes the pursuit of a goal puts the focus on things over people and can create a kind of tunnel vision where the goal becomes the major focus. As a result, the goal setter gets blindsided. Sometimes this narrow focus and impersonal pursuit of goals can even have fatal results.

When goal setters fail to put goals in proper perspective, the human factor gets set aside. For example, in the early 1990s, Sears set a sales target for its auto repair staff of $147 per hour. The energetic pursuit of the goal by mechanics, however, caused them to perform unnecessary repairs and to overcharge their customers. In the long run, what looked like a logical goal turned out to be a customer-relations nightmare for the giant retailer. Setting goals is certainly not all bad, but when setting a goal, it is important to think through consequences, both intended and possible unintended ones.

It is vital that people watch what is going on around them on the way to their destination. Too often goal setting becomes like putting on blinders, narrowing our focus and preventing us from seeing the big picture. In a 1999 study, psychologists Daniel Simons and Christopher Chabris instructed their subjects to watch a video clip. In the video, a group of people passed a basketball, and the subjects were told to count the number of passes. The results of the study showed that the majority of the participants focused so hard on their counting goal that they did not even see a woman dressed in a gorilla suit who walked through the middle of the group in the video. The problem is not that goal setting doesn't work. Instead, the problem is that goal setting can work in ways we never intended. As stated by Adam Galinsky, a professor at Northwestern University's Kellogg School of Management, "It can focus attention too much, or on the wrong things; it can lead to crazy behaviors to get people to achieve them." The blind pursuit of a goal can result in being blindsided on the road to achievement.

Evidence shows that not putting goal setting into proper perspective can cause us to lose touch with reality and maybe even our lives. In the 1960s, for example, the Ford Motor Company came up with a plan to regain the market share it was losing to foreign companies who were producing smaller cars. It set a goal to create a car that would weigh less than 2,000 pounds and cost less than $2,000 by 1970. Ford met its goal, creating the Ford Pinto, but in its rush to meet the goal, company executives failed to fully consider safety. The location of the Pinto's fuel tank, behind the rear axle, made it prone to igniting upon impact, and fifty-three people died as a result. More flexibility and a less rigid pursuit of Ford's goal would have saved lives. Realizing that goals can constrict thinking and blind us to both positive and negative outcomes is the first step toward creating goals that are flexible enough to serve us rather than making us slaves and possibly even corpses.

When misused, a goal is like putting on blinders while driving down the freeway: you may reach your destination, but you're just as likely to get sideswiped. Proper goal setting involves being circumspect enough to realize that there are blind spots on the way to your destination.

Version B

Goal setting is overrated. The pursuit of a goal puts the focus on things over people and can create a kind of tunnel vision where the goal becomes the major focus. As a result, the goal setter gets blindsided. Sometimes this narrow focus and impersonal pursuit of goals can even have fatal results.

When goal setters fail to put goals in proper perspective, the human factor gets set aside. Sometimes big corporations focus so much on making money that they fail to focus on their customers. Setting goals is certainly not all bad, but when setting a goal, it is important to think through consequences, both intended and possible unintended ones.

Goal setting can also make people focus so much on reaching a goal that they fail to see what is going on around them. A student, for example, might be so focused on getting a good grade in a class that he or she fails to put priority on learning the material. That student might go through the motions of learning, but real learning doesn't happen because the focus is on the wrong goal.

Goal setting can also be fatal. If you are climbing a mountain and you focus so much on reaching the summit, you might ignore other dangers around you. When you do this you might slip and fall or you might fail to keep track of time or to notice that a dangerous storm is approaching.

Goals are overrated because they cause us to focus too much on the goal rather than on people. They are also overrated because they cause us to focus so much on the long-term goal that we miss things along the way. They are also overrated because they can be fatal.

Version C

What does the scarcity of cabs on a rainy day have to do with goal setting? Well, as it turns out, there is a clear connection. A 1992 study found that each day cabbies set a goal of how much money they will make. On rainy days, because fewer people want to walk, cabbies make their goal amount early in the day. As a result, they take the rest of the day off, leaving potential customers standing in the rain. This absence of cabs illustrates that even though many people see goals as important tools to success, there is actually a dark side to goal setting that brings about an undesirable effect.

Goal setting is not necessarily a bad thing, but it is overrated. This is because sometimes the pursuit of a goal puts the focus on things over people and can create a kind of tunnel vision where the goal becomes the major focus. As a result, the goal setter gets blindsided. Sometimes this narrow focus and impersonal pursuit of goals can even have fatal results.

As demonstrated by the 1992 cabbie study, blind pursuit of goals can leave people out in the rain. The cabbies in the study placed cash over customer service. When goal setters fail to put goals in proper perspective, the human factor gets set aside. For example, in the early 1990s, Sears set a sales target for its auto repair staff of $147 per hour. The energetic pursuit of the goal by mechanics, however, caused them to perform unnecessary repairs and to overcharge their customers. In the long run, what looked like a logical goal turned out to be a customer-relations nightmare for the giant retailer. Setting goals is certainly not all bad, but when setting a goal, it is important to think through consequences, both intended and possible unintended ones.

In addition to watching out for the unintended consequences at the end of the road, it's also vital for people to watch what is going on around them on the way to their destinations. Too often, goal setting becomes like putting on blinders, narrowing our focus and preventing us from seeing the big picture. In a 1999 study, for examples, psychologists Daniel Simons and Christopher Chabris instructed their subjects to watch a video clip. In the video a group of people passed a basketball, and the subjects were told to count the number of passes.

The results of the study showed that the majority of the participants focused so hard on their counting goal that they did not even see a woman dressed in a gorilla suit who walked through the middle of the group in the video. The problem is not that goal setting doesn't work. Instead, the problem is that goal setting can work in ways we never intended. As stated by Adam Galinsky, a professor at Northwestern University's Kellogg School of Management, "It can focus attention too much, or on the wrong things; it can lead to crazy behaviors to get people to achieve them." The blind pursuit of a goal can result in being blindsided on the road to achievement.

Sometimes being blindsided can be fatal, and evidence shows that not putting goal setting into proper perspective can cause us to lose touch with reality and maybe even our lives. In the 1960s, for example, the Ford Motor Company came up with a plan to regain the market share it was losing to foreign companies who were producing smaller cars. It set a goal to create a car that would weigh less than 2,000 pounds and cost less than $2,000 by 1970.

Ford met its goal, creating the Ford Pinto, but in its rush to meet the goal, company executives failed to fully consider safety. The location of the Pinto's fuel tank, behind the rear axle, made it prone to igniting upon impact, and fifty-three people died as a result. More flexibility and a less rigid pursuit of Ford's goal would have saved lives.

Another example of the fatal pursuit of goals is documented in Jon Krakauer's book Into Thin Air, the story of the 1996 climbing disaster on Mt. Everest in which eight climbers lost their lives. Completely fixated on the goal of shepherding their paying customers to the summit of the world's highest mountain, the climbing party's guides ignored the warning signs of an approaching storm. Realizing that goals can constrict thinking and blind us to both positive and negative outcomes is the first step toward creating goals that are flexible enough to serve us rather than making us slaves and possibly even corpses.

When misused, a goal is like putting on blinders while driving down the freeway: You may reach your destination, but you're just as likely to get sideswiped. Proper goal setting involves being circumspect enough to realize that there are blind spots on the way to your destination. So, when you're looking for a cab on a rainy day, remember even farsighted goals can sometimes bring about shortsighted results.

Six-point Writing Rubric

6 **OUTSTANDING** (Advanced)	▪ Ideas are cogent, credible, and original. The main point is clear and well-supported, with detailed writing showing evidence, examples, and anecdotes. ▪ Word choice is skillful, sophisticated, concrete, and concise, with vivid verbs and concrete nouns from the bottom rung of the Ladder of Abstraction. ▪ Organization is coherent and complete with a clear beginning, middle, and end. An opening hook and a full-circle conclusion along with sophisticated use of signal words guide the reader from beginning to end. ▪ Voice is sincere, compelling, and creative. Includes vivid images, as well as figurative, lively, and resonant language. ▪ Sentences are fluent, varied, and clear. The writer demonstrates sophisticated control of syntax and mastery of conventions.
5 **EFFECTIVE** (Advanced/Proficient)	▪ Ideas are cogent and clear. The main point is clear, and well-supported, with showing evidence, examples, anecdotes, and details. ▪ Word choice is effective, concrete, and concise, using vivid verbs and concrete nouns from the bottom rung of the Ladder of Abstraction. ▪ Organization is coherent and complete with a clear beginning, middle, and end. An opening hook and a full-circle conclusion along with clear signal words guide the reader. ▪ Voice is interesting and distinctive. Includes vivid images, as well as figurative, concrete, and clear language. ▪ Sentences are fluent, varied, and clear. The writer demonstrates control of syntax and mastery of conventions.
4 **COMPETENT** (Proficient)	▪ Ideas are clear and logical. The main point is clear and supported with some examples, anecdotes, and details. ▪ Word choice is adequate, concrete, and concise, using some vivid verbs and concrete nouns from the bottom rung of the Ladder of Abstraction. ▪ Organization is coherent with a clear beginning, middle, and end. The writer uses a clear introduction and conclusion, along with clear signal words to guide the reader. ▪ Voice is clear and sometimes interesting. Includes vivid images, as well as language that is, for the most part, concrete and clear. ▪ Sentences are for the most part fluent, varied, and clear. Few errors in conventions.
3 **INADEQUATE** (Nearing Proficiency)	▪ Ideas and main point are clear but not supported enough with specific evidence, examples, anecdotes, and details. ▪ Word choice is not concise and vivid enough, drawing on few words from the bottom rung of the Ladder of Abstraction. ▪ Limited coherence limits the reader's ability to progress from the beginning to end. Limited use of signal words. ▪ Voice is clear but not fully engaged or sincere. Limited use of imagery and language. ▪ Sentences are clear for the most part but not always fluent or varied. Some errors in conventions.
2 **LIMITED** (Little Mastery)	▪ Ideas and main point are not clearly stated, nor are they adequately supported with specific evidence, examples, anecdotes, and details. ▪ Word choice is limited, and sometimes incorrect, using little concrete, vivid language. ▪ Seriously limited coherence limits the reader's ability to progress from the beginning to the end. Limited or no use of signal words. ▪ Voice is not clear, fully engaged, or sincere. Limited use of imagery and language. ▪ Some sentences are not clear or adequately varied. Numerous convention errors distract the reader and limit clarity of language.
1 **LACKING** (No Mastery)	▪ The ideas are vague and the support is inadequate. ▪ Word choice is very limited and often incorrect. ▪ Organization is disorganized and unfocused. ▪ Voice is not clear, is seriously limited, and is not fully engaged. ▪ Sentences are not clear or adequately varied. Pervasive errors in conventions interfere with meaning.

Chapter 14 Teaching Notes

SCORING ESSAYS WITH A RUBRIC

This activity will take approximately two class periods: one period for students to read and score the sample essays and another to report their scores and compare those scores with the actual essay scores.

Begin by giving students a copy of the writing rubric along with copies of the three essays on goal setting. Read through the rubric as a class, identifying the different levels and highlighting the differences between writing that is inadequate and writing that is adequate. Also highlight the differences between proficient writing and outstanding writing.

After students have looked at the rubric, have them individually read through the three essays and score them. Tell them to include a brief explanation of why they feel their score is accurate based on the language of the writing rubric. The process of reading through the rubric and scoring the essays individually will take at least one class period.

Next, students discuss their scores with each other in small groups. Appoint a recorder to take notes to summarize the group's main comments and average scores on each essay. Let students know that the goal of their discussion is not to simply identify a single "correct" score. Instead, the goal is to become comfortable with the scoring criteria through discussion of writing samples. Give students one class period to complete their group discussion.

During the next class period, groups share. As the groups report their scores to you, the teacher, record their average scores on each essay so that each group can see how its scores compare with the other groups' scores. Once all groups have reported, tell students the actual scores of the essays along with the comments. Devote one class period to score reporting, and use any remaining time in the period to discuss with students how their scores compared to the actual scores of the essays.

Once students have completed this activity, have them use the rubric to score any future essays they write. Scoring their own essays, and the essays written by their peers, will help them to see that the criteria for evaluating an essays is not based on a teacher's subjective judgment. Instead, the criteria from the rubric are based on the specific qualities of good writing. Knowing and using these criteria will also help students understand explicitly what they can do to improve their writing and how they can reach the highest standards of writing.

Essay Scores

Version A

Score: 4

> Comments: *This essay has a clear thesis and some specific, showing examples. More specific examples and concrete language would improve the essay. The essay also lacks a strong opening hook and transitions between paragraphs are not strong. The essay's voice is good, but more concrete language and examples would make it stronger. The essay's sentence structure is good and the writer's control of conventions is strong.*

Version B

Score: 2

> Comments: *This essay has a clear point but lacks specific, showing examples. There are some general examples, but the writer needs to elaborate with more specific examples along with more language on the bottom rung of the Ladder of Abstraction. The essay's voice is not engaging because of the lack of concrete and figurative language. The essay lacks an opening hook and signal words to guide the reader from beginning to end. Sentence variety and conventions are adequate.*

Version C

Score: 6

> Comments: *This essay has a clear thesis supported with detailed supporting examples and evidence. The word choice is sophisticated and concrete with a number of ideas from the bottom rung of the Ladder of Abstraction. The essay has a strong opening hook and a full-circle argument; effective transitions and signal words guide the reader from beginning to end. The voice of the essay is sincere and engaging, including use of figurative language. The sentence structure is fluent, varied, and clear. The writer demonstrates mastery of conventions.*

CHAPTER 15

Extra Skill-sharpening Games and Activities for the Whole Class

This chapter contains a number of resources that reinforce the exercises in Chapters 1–14.

These activities will allow you to review, revisit, and sharpen your students' ability to apply the style points in their own writing. Furthermore, the activities are collaborative, allowing you to have students work in pairs, small groups, or as a whole class.

STRATEGY POINTS: THE GAME

In this interactive game, students review and practice applying persuasive techniques by writing and sharing short passages. It may be used for each technique as students learn it or all at once after students have completed their study of the style points.

The Strategy Points Game is an especially effective way for students to see firsthand the effect of each style point on real readers. It also gives them valuable practice critiquing and commenting on the specific effects of good writing. For example, if you discover that students are not applying enough of the figurative language strategy points in their essays, you might review metaphors, similes, personification, and allusions using the game as a platform for students to reacquaint themselves with these strategies.

The game may be played in small groups (three or more), or as a whole-class activity.

Object of the Game

- To practice writing on demand under timed conditions.
- To practice applying the writing strategies.
- To write sentences so good that the judge selects them as the best.
- To focus on the qualities of outstanding writing.

Materials Needed

- A list of writing topics (see "Resources")
- Half-sheets of paper or note cards for each player
- A clock or stop watch

Directions

1. Begin by selecting a judge. If playing in a small group, select the person with the earliest birthday. If the whole class is playing the game, the teacher may play the role of judge or appoint one or more judges. Instruct judges to stay positive, commenting only on what stood out as positive traits of the writing. In other words, why did this particular piece of writing attract his/her interest? Using a panel of judges is a good way to allow more students to play the role of judge. One judge for every six students in the class is a good judge-to-player ratio.

2. The judge randomly selects one of the strategy points from the following list and one of the "101 Writing Prompts" in the "Resources" section.

Alliteration	Allusions
Anaphora	Anecdotes
Antithesis	Claims and premises
Concrete nouns	Examples
Hyphenated modifiers	Lists
Metaphors and similes	Parallelism
Personification	Vivid verbs
Zeugma	

The judge then announces to the group/class the strategy point and the writing topic that have been selected. For example, the judge would announce: "The strategy point is metaphor. The topic is: *Is the justice system in America today corrupt or fair? Does everyone, whether rich or poor, have an equal chance of achieving justice under our current system?*"

3. The players are given five minutes to write at least one sentence that relates to the announced topic featuring the announced strategy point. They write their names on one side of their papers and their sentences on the other side. The judge does not write but is responsible for keeping time and announcing to the writers when one minute is remaining.

4. Once time is up, players pass their papers to the judge, who mixes up the papers so that the identities of the writers remain secret.

5. Without looking at the names on the back of the papers, the judge reads each piece of writing aloud, pausing after each one, but not commenting at all at this point.

6. After reading each piece of writing, the judge then selects the winning entry by announcing the name of the writer, reading the winning piece of writing aloud a second time, and commenting briefly on why the selection was made. The winner is then awarded a point. Winning entries must be on the announced topic, must feature the announced strategy point, and must be written as at least one complete sentence.

7. Small groups: The person with the next earliest birthday becomes the judge, and the past judge now becomes a player. Each round is complete once each person in the group has had an opportunity to be the judge.

Whole class: New judges are selected, and the past judges become players in the next round.

Example

Here is an example of one round of play in a small group of four players.

Topic
Is the justice system in America today corrupt or fair? Does everyone, whether rich or poor, have an equal chance of achieving justice under our current system?

Style Point
Metaphor

Player 1
The justice system is a wide river that someday all of us must cross. We may feel like we are safe on solid, dry ground today, but tomorrow we may find ourselves faced with fording the swift current. Facing the reality of the American justice system is the first step in being prepared to cross it successfully.

Player 2
There are three essential tools that any great judge must pack in his satchel each day as he prepares for work: a wooden gavel, a black robe, and a trained mind.

Player 3
The scales of justice, the rule of law, the jury box—these are the three pillars that support the ceiling of justice that protects us all.

Player 4
The justice system is a mess—a festering cesspool that must be drained and cleaned up if we are to have any hope of fulfilling the promise of the U.S. Constitution.

<u>Judge's Decision</u>

I select Player 2's entry: "There are three essential tools that any great judge must pack in his satchel each day as he prepares for work: a wooden gavel, a black robe, and a trained mind." The sentence is clear, concise, and contains some good concrete images as well as word play. As well as a good metaphor, it also features a nice dramatic use of parallelism to conclude the sentence.

COLLABORATIVE WRITING ACTIVITY: TONE FOR TWO

In this activity, students work in pairs, using tone and diction to explore a writing topic. You may use this writing activity any time, but it is especially effective when students are beginning an essay to assist them in really committing to a topic, as well as when they are exploring the topic from both sides of the question.

George Orwell said, "The great enemy of clear language is insincerity." In other words, if the writer doesn't care about the topic, there is no way the reader is going to care. The secret to creating writing that the writer and the reader care about is tone, the writer's attitude toward his/her topic or audience. As Orwell warned, the writer's tone must never be insincere; it must be sincere—that is, the writer must sound like he or she cares deeply about the topic.

Even if a student is given a topic that he or she cares little about, tone is an excellent way of establishing a sincere voice by adopting a specific tone, whether positive or negative.

The following activity gives students practical experience adopting a variety of tones to write about specific topics. It's also a great pre-writing exercise that you can use to get students invested in a writing task. Doing this activity will help students see that injecting attitude into their writing will help them write with more specificity and energy. Doing so will produce more interesting and inviting writing.

Directions

1. Have students work in pairs, labeling themselves Partner A and Partner B.

2. Select one of the topics from "101 Writing Prompts" from the "Resources" section, and write it on the board.

   For example: *What is the best movie genre (drama, action, documentary, etc.)? What makes it so great?*

3. Write down a list of positive-tone adjectives and a list of negative-tone adjectives.

POSITIVE-TONE ADJECTIVES	NEGATIVE-TONE ADJECTIVES
celebratory	*alarmist*
enthusiastic	*annoyed*
excited	*bitter*
humorous	*critical*
praiseworthy	*sarcastic*

4. Instruct Partner A to write a claim and a premise, stating his/her position on the question.

   For example: *Action and adventure is the best movie genre because it keeps the viewer's interest from beginning to end.*

5. Instruct Partner B to argue against Partner A's claim and premise by adopting a negative tone. Students should write a short paragraph (at least three sentences). Encourage students to use any of the strategy points that will contribute to the tone. You might suggest some as well as have students suggest some, such as specific examples, metaphor, personification, hyphenated modifiers, or parallelism.

> Here's an example of a response with a critical tone.
> *Action films pander to the pathetic public by giving them cheap thrills but no substance. Car chases, flying bullets, and exploding buildings are no substitute for real character development. No wonder they have to keep making new* Die Hard, Terminator, *and* Indiana Jones *movies. Like cotton candy, action films offer no nutritional value and simply leave you craving more of the sticky, sugary pap that melts to nothing.*

6. Instruct Partner A to argue for the claim and premise by adopting a positive tone.

> Here's an example of a response with an excited tone.
> *I'll never forget the first time I watched* Die Hard *on the big screen. Every machine gun blast, every broken window, every twist and turn of the plot kept me riveted. I was so mesmerized for the two hours of the film that I hardly moved a muscle or even blinked. No other film genre offers this kind of excitement and intensity of experience. It's what movies were meant to do: grab you by the collar and transport you from the mundane world to the magical, majestic world of non-stop action and adventure. Sure, it's not real, but that's exactly what makes it so appealing.*

7. When both students have written their paragraphs, have them read them aloud to the class. Instruct students to listen for the specific negative and positive tones. Challenge students to see if they can pinpoint the specific tone adjective for each paragraph.

8. After completing the activity, make sure to explain to students that tone is an excellent way to trick themselves into writing sincerely about any topic, even one in which they have very little interest. In many testing situations, they will be given a single topic to write about, and chances are they will one day meet up with a topic that they don't feel sincerely about. Tone will allow them to adopt an attitude that they can use to avoid sounding insincere.

PART III

Resources

This section contains materials that you can use as reference materials for your students.

First, the "Review and Revision Reminders" summarizes each of the style points, with brief definitions, examples, and explanations. Once students have been introduced to each of the style points, you might reproduce these reminders for them so that they can refer to them in future writing assignments.

Second, a list called "101 Writing Prompts" is provided so that you and your students will never be at a loss for possible writing topics. Each question is stated to elicit an opinionated response that students can support with reasoning, evidence, and detail.

Third, a glossary of terms is provided so that you and your students can quickly find definitions of key terms along with examples to illustrate them.

STUDENT HANDOUT: REVIEW AND REVISION REMINDERS

Keep and use this handout as a ready reference to review the writing strategies you have learned. Also use it during revision for specific examples of how each of the strategies you have learned will improve your writing.

Ideas and Details

1. **Thesis with a claim and premises.** Make sure your thinking is clear by using a thesis that gives your reader a roadmap of your essay, a roadmap that provides a claim and premises. Make sure that every paragraph and every sentence of your writing is relevant to proving your thesis. Because your reader comes first, state your claim and your premises clearly.

    Original: *Anacortes, Washington, is a great place to live.*

    Revised: *Anacortes, Washington, is a great place to live because of its beautiful forestlands, its small town feel, and its low crime rate.*

2. **Counterarguments.** Build credibility with your reader by anticipating opposing arguments to your thesis and rebutting them with your sound reasoning.

    Original: *Gambling should not be legalized because it causes communities to lose tax revenues from the increased crime and bankruptcies that result from legal gambling.*

    Revised: *Although some people argue that gambling increases tax revenues for a community, the reality is that it decreases revenues because of the increased crime and bankruptcies that come to any community that adopts legal gambling.*

3. **Examples.** A thesis tells, but examples show; good writing does both, so include relevant, specific examples. Whether you use deductive reasoning or inductive reasoning, make sure that you balance the abstract with the concrete and the general with the specific by giving your reader detailed examples.

    Original: *Computers have come a long way in the past sixty years.*

    Revised: *Computers have come a long way; for example, today's musical greeting card is more powerful than the world's most powerful computer was sixty years ago.*

4. **Anecdotes.** People were telling stories long before they were writing anything down. As a result, your reader is predisposed to enjoy a good yarn, especially if it is relevant to illustrating your point. Use anecdotes to make your writing more concrete, more captivating, and more compelling. Even a brief anecdote can go a long way to making your point.

> Original: *In preparing a speech, remember to make brief notes.*

> Revised: *In preparing his "Gettysburg Address," Abraham Lincoln wrote his ideas out on the back of an envelope. Great speeches begin with ordinary preparation.*

5. **Persuasive appeals and details.** Appeal to your reader's logic and reason (*logos*), imagination and emotions (*pathos*), and need to trust your credibility and character (*ethos*). Use showing details, like statistics, dialogue, and quotations to support your point and persuade with style.

> Logos and statistics: *Even* The New York Times *has trouble with spelling. Since the year 2000, America's newspaper of record has misspelled the word "misspelled" fourteen times.*

> Pathos and dialogue: *People waste too much time worrying about spelling. For example, as I'm writing this essay, instead of thinking carefully about my ideas, I'm wasting time thinking about things like, "How do you spell 'carefully' again? Is it with or without an 'e'?"*

> Ethos and quotations: *Napoleon Bonaparte, the great French emperor and military leader, did not rank spelling very high on his list of priorities, saying, "A man occupied with public or other important business cannot, and need not attend to spelling."*

Diction

6. **Vivid verbs.** Comb your draft to make sure that your verbs give your reader specific, vivid pictures (and possibly sounds). Favor action verbs (*glare*, *limp*, *whisper*) over state-of-being verbs (*is*, *was*, *were*), and favor the active voice over the passive.

> Original: *The student was told by the teacher to sit down.*

> Revised: *The teacher's voice thundered as he barked at the student to sit down.*

7. **Concrete nouns.** Make sure that you provide your reader with concrete nouns from the bottom rung of the Ladder of Abstraction (Rung 4: *Person*, Rung 3: *Student*, Rung 2: *Sophomore*, Rung 1: *Bill O'Neill*). Have you included nouns that can be touched or felt by your hand? *Tell* with abstract, general nouns, but *show* with concrete, specific nouns.

> Original: *My grandfather recited poetry as he did his chores.*

> Revised: *As a boy in the 1940s, I stood in the tie-up watching my New Hampshire grandfather milk Holsteins while reciting poems for my entertainment. His hands stripped milk to the poem's beat. He threw back his head, rolled his eyes in high drama and pounded out: "But there is no joy in Mudville—mighty Casey has struck out." —Donald Hall*

8. **Lists—asyndeton and polysyndeton.** Look for a place in your draft where you can bring your reader back to earth by including a list of specific, concrete things that he/she can see, or feel, or taste, or smell, or hear. Consider using asyndeton or polysyndeton where appropriate to make your lists resonate with your reader.

> Original: *Being a teenager means dealing with the daily slings and arrows of outrageous fortune. It's not easy being a teen.*

> Revised: *Being a teenager means dealing with the daily slings and arrows of outrageous fortune: school lunches, your dog eating your homework, too much homework, too little sleep, unrequited love, popping a zit and then forgetting to maintain it so it bleeds all over your face, paper cuts, grades posted on the Internet, bad hair days, being picked last in gym, walking into the wrong bathroom, forgetting your locker combination, not realizing that there are questions on the back of the test, testy teachers, calling someone the wrong name but not realizing it until they're gone and it's too late to correct yourself, embarrassing yearbook photos, having everything on the test be everything you didn't study, reading* Hamlet.

9. **Zeugma.** This figure of speech makes your verbs stand out and your reader stand up and take notice. With zeugma a verb does double-duty since it is employed in two entirely different senses. It's the perfect way to make your words both work and play.

> Original: *As his relationship with the girl continued, he fell madly in love, but he also began going into debt.*

> Revised: *As his relationship with the girl continued, he fell madly in love and deeper in debt.*

10. **Hyphenated modifier.** This is the anything-but-everyday device that allows you to turn the tables on typical English syntax by using concrete language to modify just about any noun. These quirky coagulations of language can add a hint of humor or a spark of sarcasm.

> Original: *He's one of those students who is always late to first period.*

> Revised: *He's one of those I-never-arrive-less-than-five-minutes-late-to-first-period students.*

Voice and Figurative Language

11. **Metaphors and similes.** Use metaphors and similes to make interesting comparisons that set your writing apart from the crowd. Abstract, general ideas become more concrete and vivid for your reader when you use figurative language. Shake the dust off a tired idea; use a metaphor to polish it up and make it look and sound brand new. The following examples reveal how figurative language can transform a *telling* sentence into a *showing* one.

> Original: *Maintaining a good friendship is not easy.*

> Revised with a metaphor: *Friendship is a fire that stays aflame only through constant attention.*

> Original: *A limited vocabulary can impede your progress.*

> Revised with a simile: *Limited vocabulary, like short legs on a pole-vaulter, builds in a natural barrier to progress beyond a certain point.* —John Gardner

12. **Personification.** Personification is your pal. Add life to your writing by combining the power of figurative language with the power of specific, vivid word choice. Make your words work, your sentences sing, and your paragraphs pounce.

> Original: *No one is immune to fate.*

> Revised: *There is no armor against fate; death lays his icy hands on kings.* —Jane Shirley

13. **Allusions.** Connect your writing with the timeless stories from history, mythology, and literature. Stories plus figurative language equals a powerful combination that make your sentences stand as tall as Everest.

> Original: *Foreign correspondents were a revered, much romanticized group.*

> Revised: *Foreign correspondents were a revered, much romanticized group—the Indiana Joneses of journalism.* —The New Yorker

Syntax

14. **Parallelism.** Thinking in threes will help you elaborate, illustrate, and clarify your writing. This secret weapon of great orators and writers alike will give your writing a rhythm, repetition, and resonance to make it memorable.

> Original: *His textbooks under his arm, Sam walked briskly through the cafeteria.*

> Revised: *His textbooks under his arm, his eyes focused straight ahead, and his mind preoccupied with his upcoming math test, Sam walked briskly through the cafeteria.*

15. **Antithesis.** Use antithesis to contrast ideas, to generate tension, and to create balance. Opposites attract. When ideas clash, your reader sticks around to watch the fight. A little antithesis can make a big difference.

> Original: *I've done it! I'm on the moon's surface!*

> Revised: *That's one small step for man; one giant leap for mankind.* —Neil Armstrong

16. **Alliteration.** Look for a sentence in your draft where you can apply the powerful punch provided by alliteration. In moderation, alliteration will accentuate an idea and add eloquence.

> Original: *Every passing week brings news for coffee lovers, and the latest news is the best yet.*

> Revised: *Every passing week brings news for latte lovers, and the latest on coffee is the best buzz yet.* —Kathleen McAuliffe

17. **Anaphora.** Used in the right way, at the right time, and at the right place in a paragraph, anaphora is the rhetorical re-run that adds a powerful punch to your ideas. Whether you echo at the beginning of a sentence, at the beginning of a clause, or at the beginning of a phrase, anaphora will energize your ideas.

> Original: *We shall fight on the beaches and landing grounds, in the streets and the hills.*

> Revised: *We shall fight on the beaches, we shall fight on the landing grounds, we shall fight in the streets, we shall fight in the hills, we shall never surrender.* —Winston Churchill

Organization

18. **Signal words.** It's the writer's job to get the reader from the beginning to the end of a composition as smoothly and seamlessly as possible. Use signal words— transition words (*such as*, *for example*, *however*, *therefore*, *because*), repeated words, synonyms, and pronouns—as signposts for the reader, showing how ideas within and between sentences relate. Signal words also create logical links and easy transitions between paragraphs.

> *July 20, 1969, is a pivotal date in the history of technological advancement. On that day Neil Armstrong walked on the moon, an unparalleled human achievement that demonstrated the ability of technology to transport and liberate humankind from its limits. That same day back on earth another miraculous demonstration of technological advancement was the fact that Americans were able to sit in their living rooms, watching and listening on television as Armstrong took his first steps. Television made it possible for millions of Americans to be eye-witnesses to a milestone in the history of humanity, demonstrating its potential power to inform, inspire, and unite. Four decades after that first moonwalk, however, television's promise has fallen well short of its potential. Instead of informing, it has become a distraction. Instead of inspiring, it has deadened thought. Instead of uniting, it has isolated people.*

19. **Opening hook.** Make a strong first impression on your reader by beginning on the first rung of the Ladder of Abstraction, talking about concrete, specific people, places, and things. Consider using an inductive hook, a concrete noun hook, a figurative language hook, or an alliterative antithesis hook.

> *What does the scarcity of cabs on a rainy day have to do with goal setting? Well, as it turns out, there is a clear connection. A 1992 study found that each day cabbies set a goal of how much money they will make. On rainy days, because fewer people want to walk, cabbies make their goal amount early in the day. As a result, they take the rest of the day off, leaving potential customers standing in the rain. This absence of cabs illustrates that even though many people see goals as important tools to success, there is actually a dark side to goal setting that brings about an undesirable effect. Goal setting in not necessarily a bad thing, but it is overrated. This is because sometimes the pursuit of a goal puts the focus on things over people, and can create a kind of tunnel vision where the goal becomes the major focus; as a result, the goal setter gets blindsided. Sometimes this narrow focus and impersonal pursuit of goals can even have fatal results.*

20. **Conclusions.** Make a strong last impression by rephrasing, rather than just restating, your thesis. Then, use a clincher in your final sentence to end with a punch. Use either an anaphora clincher to create an echo effect or a full-circle clincher to return your reader to your opening image or ideas.

> *When misused, a goal is like putting on blinders while driving down the freeway: you may reach your destination, but you're just as likely to get sideswiped. Proper goal setting involves being circumspect enough to realize that there are blind spots on the way to your destination. So when you're looking for a cab on a rainy day, remember even far-sighted goals can sometimes bring about shortsighted results.*

21. **Varied sentence length.** The best way to make your sentences imitate the natural rhythms of human speech is to use a variety of sentence lengths. It's easy. Just count up the number of words in your sentences and adjust as needed. Read your sentences aloud. Consider using a cumulative, periodic, or balanced sentence where appropriate to add snap to your syntax. Read the following two passages aloud. See if you notice a difference.

> Original: *Once upon a time any writer worth his or her salt carried a knife. Why would a bard brandish a knife or a writer wield a weapon? Please tell me that this legend is not true, Shakespeare! Before metal-tipped pens, the only writing tool available was a feather—or quill. Quill pens wore down quickly, so scribes carried a sharpening tool known as a "penknife." In fact, the word "pen" derives from the Latin word "penna," meaning quill.*

> Revised: *Once upon a time, any writer worth his or her salt carried a knife. Bards brandishing blades? Writers wielding weapons? Say it isn't so, Shakespeare! Well, in an age before metal-tipped pens, ballpoint pens, or typewriters, the only writing tool available was a feather—or quill. These quill pens wore down quickly. Because of this, every scribe carried a sharpening tool, a blade known as a "penknife." In fact, the word "pen" derives from the Latin word "penna," meaning quill.*

22. **Deductive and inductive organization.** Usually writers tell the reader their point and then show that it is true by supporting it with details, moving from the general to the specific. This is deductive organization. Sometimes, however, it makes sense to begin by showing and to end with telling, moving from specific to general details. This is called inductive organization.

> Deductive: *Emergencies have always been necessary to progress. It was darkness which produced the lamp. It was fog that produced the compass. It was hunger that drove us to exploration. And it took a depression to teach us the real value of a job.*

> Inductive: *It was darkness which produced the lamp. It was fog that produced the compass. It was hunger that drove us to exploration. And it took a depression to teach us the real value of a job. Emergencies have always been necessary to progress.*

Student Handout Review and Revision Reminders

101 WRITING PROMPTS

The following 101 questions are designed to give you, the teacher, and your students many possible persuasive writing topics. Any of the questions would be suitable as an assigned essay question or a persuasive paragraph. In addition, each question is broad enough to elicit a variety of possible persuasive responses.

1. **Activities:** What activity do you most enjoy? Convince someone else to participate in that activity.
2. **Advice:** What one piece of advice would you give to someone younger than yourself about success in life?
3. **Advice:** What is the single best piece of advice you ever got? Why was it so helpful?
4. **Ads:** Which single commercial or advertisement would you say is the most successful? Why?
5. **Ads:** What is the single most effective appeal used in advertisements? Why is it so effective?
6. **Animals:** What one behavior/instinct of a specific animal provides the best example for human success?
7. **Americans:** Who would you argue is the greatest American? Why?
8. **Anachronisms:** What is something that people do or use today that is outdated? Why should this activity or thing be placed in the dustbin of history?
9. **Annual events:** What one annual event do you think everyone should attend? Why is it such a great event? Describe it.
10. **Awards:** What single new award would you create? Why or how does your award recognize a significant achievement?
11. **Behavior:** What is something that people do that you find rude? Why do you feel it is rude and why do you think people should avoid it?
12. **Belief:** What is the single most important thing you believe? Write a "This I Believe" editorial explaining what you believe and why.
13. **Books:** What one book should be on the required reading list of life? Why is it so important?
14. **Capital punishment:** Should the death penalty remain legal in the U.S.? Why or why not?
15. **Careers:** What is the single most important factor in selecting a career?
16. **Causes:** What is a cause that you believe is worth supporting? Convince your reader why it is so important.
17. **City or small town:** Which is the better place to live: a large city or a small town? Why?
18. **Cell phones:** What statement would you make positively or negatively about cell phones? Make and support your claim with evidence and examples.
19. **Change:** If you had the power to change one thing in America tomorrow to make it a better place, what would you change?
20. **Change:** If you were to change one thing about yourself, what would you change and why?
21. **Competition:** Is competition important, or should everyone be allowed to win? Make your case.
22. **Community service:** Should schools require students to perform community service, or should it be purely voluntary?

23. **Criticism:** If you were to go on a rant, criticizing something, what would it be? Why is this person, place, thing, or idea so bad?

24. **Discipline:** What is the single most effective method for disciplining children? Why is it effective?

25. **Driving:** What is the most important aspect of driver safety?

26. **Education:** Is single-sex education a good idea, or should boys and girls remain together in the classroom?

27. **Education:** What is the most essential tool for a student? Why is it so important?

28. **Education:** What is something that is not taught in school that should be? Why?

29. **Environment:** What is one thing that you would argue that everyone can and should do help the environment?

30. **Fear:** What is one specific thing that people fear that they shouldn't? Explain why this fear is unnecessary and how to overcome it.

31. **Fictional characters:** What one fictional character offers the best example/ guidance on how to live a successful, productive life?

32. **Field trips:** Are field trips for students a waste of money, or are they actually excellent learning experiences?

33. **Food:** What is the most underrated or overrated food? Why?

34. **Games:** What is the greatest game ever invented? What makes it so great?

35. **Goals:** What is one thing you would like to accomplish before you die? Why?

36. **Grades:** Which is more important: grades or learning?

37. **Habits:** What is a habit (physical, emotional, or financial) that everyone should develop and practice? Why is it a good habit?

38. **Habits:** What bad habit (physical, emotional, or financial) should people break? Why is it a bad habit?

39. **Hassles:** What is the single biggest hassle of modern life?

40. **History:** What single new national holiday would you declare to celebrate a historical event, anniversary, or birthday?

41. **History:** What historic site would you like to visit? Explain why the historic event that happened there was important.

42. **History:** Is it really important to look to the past and learn from it, or is it better to live without looking back?

43. **History:** If you had the power to change any event in history, which would you choose to change and why?

44. **History:** What person from history who is no longer living has the most to teach us about living a good life? What makes this person's life so exemplary?

45. **Hometown:** Imagine your job is to attract visitors to your hometown. Why should they visit or move there?

46. **Internet:** What is the single best thing on the Internet? What makes it so great?

47. **Justice:** Is the justice system in America today corrupt or fair? Does everyone, whether rich or poor, have an equal chance at achieving justice under our current system?

48. **Laws:** If you could establish a single law, what would it be and why?

49. **Leadership:** What is the most important trait of a good leader? Why?

50. **Learning:** Is learning for learning's sake important or should all learning have a practical application?

51. **Man-made objects:** What is the single most beautiful or impressive man-made object? What makes it so great?

52. **Marriage:** What is the single most important component in maintaining a healthy, lifelong marriage? Why is this component important?

53. **Media:** Does the media simply report the news or does the media (newspapers, magazines, TV, radio, movies, and the Internet) shape and determine what people think and value?

54. **Military service:** Should military service be required for all Americans, or should it remain voluntary?

55. **Money:** What is your best tip for how to effectively manage money? What is this trait important?

56. **Money:** Is the pursuit of money a virtue or a vice? Explain.

57. **Movies:** What is the single most important trait for a classic movie? Why is this trait important?

58. **Movies:** What is your all time favorite movie? Persuade your reader to watch this film.

59. **Movies:** What is the best movie genre (drama, action, documentary, etc.)? What makes it so great?

60. **Music:** If one instrument were required for all school children to learn, what one instrument would you argue should be taught? What makes this instrument so valuable?

61. **Music:** What one song would you argue is the one song that all persons should have on their iPod? What makes the song so great?

62. **Music:** What one type of music or specific musician/band should everyone listen to? Why?

63. **Nature or nurture:** Which has the most influence on the life we live: our genes or our experiences? Why?

64. **Neighbors:** What is the single most important thing an individual can do to be a good neighbor? Why is this important to do?

65. **Online communication:** Does online communication help or hurt interpersonal skills and the ability of people to have meaningful relationships with real people?

66. **Optimism:** What thing are you most optimistic about? Why?

67. **Overrated:** What one thing would you say is overrated? Why?

68. **Parents:** What is the single most important characteristic of a good parent? Why?

69. **Past or present:** Was the life of the average individual simpler fifty years ago or is it simpler today?

70. **Pets:** Is having a pet an important part of growing up? Why or why not?

71. **Places:** What is a place that you have visited that you think everyone should visit? Persuade your reader to go there.

72. **Photos:** What experience in your life would like to have a photo of? Why was it so memorable?

73. **Praise:** What one thing do you think is worth praising? Why?

74. **Problem-Solution:** What is the single biggest problem facing America today? How would you solve it?

75. **Quotations:** What one quotation do you find is the most inspirational for living your life? Why is this a great quotation to live by?

76. **Reading:** There are more things to read today than there have ever been in history. What is one specific thing that you think that everyone should read?

77. **Seasons:** Which season of the year do you anticipate the most? Why? Persuade a skeptical reader that it is the best season of the year.

78. **Sports:** What single factor is the most important in deciding whether or not to participate in a specific sport?

79. **Sports:** What sport that is currently not a sport at your high school should become an extracurricular sport? Why?

80. **Sports:** What change would you make to an existing sport to make it more interesting to play or to watch?

81. **Start:** What is something that you would like to start doing? Why?
82. **Start:** What is something that you think that people should start doing that they, in general, are not doing now? Why?
83. **Stops:** What would you like to stop doing? Why?
84. **Stops:** What do you wish that people would stop doing? Why?
85. **Success:** What would you argue is the single most important attribute of a successful person? Why?
86. **Tasks:** What is one of life's most unpleasant tasks? What makes it so terrible?
87. **Technology:** What is the single best or worse change in life that has been brought about by technology in the past twenty-five years? Explain why it has specifically made life better or worse.
88. **Television:** What would you argue is the best thing that has ever been on television? What makes it so great?
89. **Television:** What would you are argue is the worst thing that has ever been on television? What makes it so bad?
90. **Television:** Does watching violence on TV, movies, or video games lead to violent acts?
91. **Television:** Is watching TV helpful or harmful?
92. **Thinking:** What is the single most important type of thinking that humans do? Define it clearly and explain why it is so important.
93. **Themes:** What is the single most important theme in literature? Give examples of this theme in various stories/works of literature that show why it is so important.
94. **Time travel:** If you had a choice to travel to the past or to the future, which would you chose? Why?
95. **Travel:** What is the best means of travel: foot, car, plane, train, or other?
96. **Tribute:** What one person would you say has made a difference in making the world a better place? What have they done specifically?
97. **Toys:** What toy would you put in the Toy Hall of Fame? What makes it such a great toy?
98. **Underrated:** What one thing would you say is underrated? Why?
99. **Virtues:** What one virtue is the most important for parents to teach to their children? Why?
100. **Voting:** Is it important to vote? Why?
101. **Words:** What single word or phrase do you think should be said more often? Why?

GLOSSARY OF KEY TERMS

These terms are explained in detail in Chapters 1–13. Students should commit these definitions to memory, so it would be a good idea to have them record the definitions on note cards.

Abstract noun: An idea that can't be perceived by the senses, such as *bravery*, *dedication*, *excellence*, or *anxiety*.

Action verb: A verb that describes specific action, evoking a picture, a sound, a smell, a taste, or a feeling, such as: *scribble*, *scramble*, *weave*, *crash*, or *whistle*.

Active voice: A sentence in which the subject is the doer of the action, such as: *Bill broke the window.*

Alliteration: The repetition of initial sounds of words; for example, *You are either green and growing or ripe and rotting.*

Allusion: A reference to a person, place, or thing from history, mythology, or literature, such as *Job*, *Mount Olympus*, or *Watergate*.

Anaphora: The repetition of the initial words in phrases, clauses, or sentences, such as: *We shall fight on the beaches, we shall fight on the landing grounds, we shall fight in the streets, we shall fight in the hills, we shall never surrender.*

Anecdote: A brief story that illustrates a point.

Antithesis: The juxtaposition of contrasting ideas in parallel words, phrases, or clauses, such as: *To err is human, to forgive is divine.*

Assonance: The repetition of accented vowel sounds, as in the phrase *fit as a fiddle.*

Asyndeton: The omission of conjunctions in a series of words, phrases, or clauses, such as: *At the store we bought apples, oranges, bananas.*

Balanced sentence: A sentence in which the clauses are written in the same grammatical structure, such as: *Hate is a human emotion, but love is a human need.*

Claim: The core of an argument, a statement of opinion that the writer supports with reasoning and evidence. For example: *Gun control should be further tightened.*

Concrete noun: A person, place, or thing that can be held or touched by your hand, such as *knee-high tube socks*, *a brown bag*, or *a splash of salt water.*

Consonance: The repetition of consonant sounds, as in the phrases *odds and ends* and *last but not least.*

Cumulative sentence: A sentence that is grammatically complete before its end, such as: *Gary played Monopoly with an intensity never before seen in any high school cafeteria.* Sometimes called a "loose sentence."

Deduction: Reasoning by moving from the general to the specific.

Diction: The writer's word choice.

Ethos: The writer's ability to establish credibility with the reader. The audience will be more easily persuaded if they feel that the writer has good sense, good will, and good character.

Example: A specific detail that illustrates a generalization.

Generalization: An inference that can be supported with examples.

Hyphenated modifier: The use of hyphenated words, besides just adjectives, to modify a noun, such as: *He's one of those I-never-arrive-less-than-five-minutes-late-to-class students.*

Induction: Reasoning by moving from the specific to the general.

Logos: Persuasion by appealing to logic, reason, and structure.

Metaphor: A figurative comparison between two unrelated nouns, such as: *Friendship is a fire that stays aflame only through constant attention.*

Onomatopoeia: Words that imitate sound, such as *pop*, *bang*, or *buzz*.

Parallelism: The repetition of grammatical structure in words, phrases, or clauses. For example: *Life is a compromise of what your ego wants to do, what experience tells you to do, and what your nerves let you do.* —Bruce Crampton

Passive voice: A sentence in which the subject is the receiver of the action, such as: *The window was broken by Bill.*

Pathos: Persuasion by appealing to imagination and emotion.

Periodic sentence: A sentence that is not grammatically complete until its last phrase, such as: *Despite Glenn's hatred of his sister's laziness and noisy eating habits, <u>he still cared for her</u>.*

Personification: Figurative language in which human attributes are used to describe things, such as: *The rock stubbornly refused to move.*

Polysyndeton: An addition of conjunctions in a series of words, phrases, or clauses, such as: *At the store we bought apples and oranges and bananas.*

Premise: A reason that supports the validity of a claim. For example: *Gun control should be further tightened <u>because guns do not deter crime</u>.*

Rhetoric: The art of using written and spoken language to persuade using both reason and imagination.

Simile: A figurative comparison between two unrelated nouns using *like* or *as*, such as: *Success is like the sunshine—it brings the rattlesnakes out.*

State-of-being verb: A verb such as *is*, *am*, *was*, *were*, or *being*.

Thesis: A one-sentence statement of the writer's argument containing a claim and at least one premise.

Tone: The writer's attitude toward his/her subject or audience.

Video verb: An action verb that provides pictures for the reader, such as *scramble*, *crush*, *weave*, or *snatch*.

Volume verb: An action verb that provides a soundtrack for the reader, such as *crash*, *gulp*, *whistle*, or *splash*.

Zeugma: A figure of speech where a single verb is used in two completely different ways. For example: *As his relationship with the girl continued, he fell madly in love and deeper in debt.*

PROFESSIONAL RESOURCES

From Chapter 2, Exercise 9: Willingham, Daniel T. *Why Students Don't Like School.* San Francisco: Jossey-Bass: 2009.

From Chapter 2, Exercise 12: Goldenberg, David and Erik Vance. "10 Technologies We Stole from the Animal Kingdom." <u>Mental Floss</u> May-June 2009: 52-59.

From Chapter 3, Introduction: Bourne, Jr., Lyle E, Roger L. Dominowski, Elizabeth F. Loftus. *Cognitive Processes.* New Jersey, Prentice-Hall, 1979.

From Chapter 4, Activity 24: Hayakawa, S.I. *Language in Thought and Action* (3rd Edition). New York: Harcourt Brace Jovanovich, Inc., 1971.

From Chapter 4, Activity 26: Freeman, Dave and Neil Teplica. *100 Things to Do Before You Die.* Dallas, Texas: Taylor Publishing Company, 1999.

From Chapter 14: Bennet, Drake. "Why Setting Goals Can Backfire." *The Boston Globe* 15 March 2009.

From Chapter 14: Ordóñez, Lisa D, Maurice E. Schweitzer, Adam D. Galinsky, and Max H. Bazerman. "Goals Gone Wild: The Systematic Side Effects of Over-Prescribing Goal Setting." 11 Feb. 2009.

NOTES

NOTES

NOTES

NOTES